W9-BCJ-559

RELIGION IN ALL THE SCHOOLS

RELIGION IN ALL THE SCHOOLS

By Leo R. Ward, C.S.C.

FIDES PUBLISHERS / NOTRE DAME, INDIANA

Library of Congress Catalog Card Number: 60-15438

MAR 2 2 1961

Imprimi Potest: Theodore J. Mehling, C.S.C.
Provincial Superior

Nihil Obstat: John E. Walsh, C.S.C.
Censor Deputatus

Imprimatur: ✠ Leo A. Pursley, D.D.
Bishop of Fort Wayne

Copyright: 1960, Fides Publishers,
Notre Dame, Indiana

Manufactured by American Book-Stratford Press

Contents

Foreword

1. Freedom *v*. Fear   1
2. The Right to Religious Literacy   32
3. The Wall of Separation   57
4. Pluralism in Education   86
5. Judeo-Christian Insights   117
6. A Plan of Action   146

Foreword

To raise the question of religion in American schools is sure to alarm the standpatter. The very phrase "religion in education" will alert him and he will feel as if he was being attacked by an enemy from Mars. All the same, we have to admit first and last that the standpatter is holding to a good principle. He is telling us to have some common sense and to let sleeping dogs lie. Let bad enough alone.

We are going to buck this interesting man though we know that on the present question the woods are full of just his type. Let him and his brethren get scared. That will be so much gained, since sometimes to get a good scare is a good thing. It depends on the occasion and the issue, and on God and religion in American education we have the issue and have reached the occasion.

Before we take the plunge into such icy waters, let us glance for a moment at some outstanding works already done or being done in the line of religion in American education. They may surprise us a little. The background consists briefly in two major facts. One is the fact that we have always had many church-related schools. That is "a fact," something solid like a stone wall. The second fact is that we have hundreds of church-related schools today on all levels from kindergarten right up, on a Jewish, a Catholic, and a Protestant basis, and Catholics at least keep on building new ones. There they are—we cannot dodge them. Private schools are as native to us as our demand for freedom and are a part and expression of that demand. Three hundred years ago they were congenital to us and of course they remain integrally a part of us.

That is the backdrop and beginning of the story. Today the nation is full of public schools somehow embodying religion in education. State colleges and universities, naturally freer than the lower grades, are teaching both religion and sectarian religion. The "Protestant non-sectarian" schools on all levels do the same thing. Some public-school teachers keep opening the school day with prayer, and many village public schools feature a verse or two from the Bible. This sort of thing is routine in the South. Elsewhere, too, officials ask schools to start the day with prayers: for instance, in New York State and in the city of St. Louis.

In the Deep South such practices are so open and so pronounced and so Protestant that they could not stand up to a trial by even a local court. For example, in North Carolina more than a hundred teachers of religion, trained in Bible schools, are employed to teach Protestant religion in public high schools. In Mississippi, children in high school must obtain a modicum of credit in "Bible," with the King James version prescribed, and they may further obtain a quarter-credit in "religion," which we are assured is taught by Protestant clergymen. Some such thing is multiplied in various ways, most notably in the South.

Then, whatever our theories and whatever our desires,

some teaching of religion is involved in context, for example
in teaching poetry and history, and for the sake of objective
scientific honesty this teaching of religion in context must
be allowed and encouraged in all schools. Good and free
teachers always face up to everything contained in the
matters they teach. Also an old idea, that of a Judeo-Christian philosophy and even of a general Judeo-Christian
learning, has again declared itself and progressively finds
a place in the sun. At least as ancient as St. Augustine, for
two generations this idea has been revived by scholars,
above all in France, and has spread to alert and living minds
in all of Europe and in North and South America. This
idea is technical and radical. It is also novel and shocking
to minds of the single-track variety, and we must attempt
to clarify it in a special chapter. Just now we make two
remarks: first, this is an idea which scholars are duty-bound
at least to examine, and second, if grasped and realized,
the idea might give American public and private schools
a needed shot in the arm.

Events of another type are pointing in a positive direction in this matter of religion in American schools. Take
three of these events. The U.S. Supreme Court decision in
the Zorach case (1952) made things simpler for the whole
question of "religion in the schools" and was in effect
though certainly not in intention a possible opening wedge.
Writing up the majority opinion in that decision, Justice
Douglas said that a friendly view of religion in relation
to public schools is entirely in the cards so far as freedom
and the American way are concerned. Secondly, subsequent
to and consequent on the McCollum decision by the same
Court (1948), expert and scholarly studies by men who
know their law and their Constitution have made many,
perhaps even some on the Supreme Bench, think that the
McCollum decision, outlawing the teaching of religion in

public schools, was biased and ill-founded. In passing let us name some of those experts and their universities: Corwin of Princeton, Cushman of Illinois, Katz of Chicago, Kauper of Michigan, and Sutherland of Cornell (now of Harvard). Thirdly, our armed forces at home and abroad have gone on independently seeing to religion for their children in public schools. In Germany, for example, the forces have been teaching the teachers of Jewish, Catholic, and Protestant religions, and the Army has been paying for all of this out of the taxpayer's pocket. An "anti" as bold and secularist as Paul Blanshard hesitates to make war on the Army.

That, briefly, is one side of the picture. What is going on is a kind of osmosis, most of it unofficial and almost entirely off the record. But slight and tame as all this certainly is, we must say that American education is not only beginning to do something about religion in education, but is far freer and more daring and constructive on the matter than is British education. That is, if we are to credit the word of Sir Walter Moberly in *The Crisis in Education*. The most that Sir Walter and others hope for, at least in the universities, is furtive infiltration. That, of course, has long gone on in American schools and universities. But events have proved that we can do better than that.

At the same time, we suffer restrictions and hobbles as impressive as the things being done. Even if we can conceive of a Christian university, as Sir Walter says the British cannot, we have real and formidable handicaps that are in part peculiar to us. For the moment we merely mention three of these: the "separation" principle, habit, and fear of each other. The first and the third will be developed and the second subsumed in the text.

Let us return to the positive. Some studies of the situation have long been under way. Prompted in the first place by the National Conference of Christians and Jews, studies have been made for over twenty years by the American Council on Education. The purpose has been to see where Americans stand on this problem of religion in public schools and to explore difficulties and possibilities.

Dr. F. Ernest Johnson, the distinguished Protestant clergyman and educator who has been chairman of the committee making the studies, has said that what we seek is "a better solution of the religious problem in the curriculum of public education." In this book and out of it we seek that "better solution." But we must seek more because the times and the situation demand more. What we must seek is a comprehensive solution of the problem of education in religious literacy in all American schools on all levels, and no matter what the public or private label on particular schools. This is a total problem and is not to be isolated from this or that type of school and segregated in other types. Dr. Johnson has added that such a solution as he suggests * is "the only answer to the religious school" in this connection. We are not looking for an answer to the religious school, and again we take Dr. Johnson himself to be unduly narrow in his conception of the problem. In fact, we must look to the religious school, perhaps a greatly improved religious school, for part of the answer. At bottom we are not looking for an answer to a school, but looking, perhaps too optimistically, for an answer, partly through the schools, to a national problem. The problem is such that we must take a full-length American view of it. Ours is a pluralist society, and for that reason we are unwilling to settle for anything short of a comprehensive answer.

It is a pleasure to thank the many friends who have

* See F. Ernest Johnson, "Religion and Public Education." *Current Religious Thought,* Febr. 1950, p. 23.

helped in the effort to open up this subject, though of course views expressed are mine and not necessarily theirs. I am especially grateful to Dr. Herman E. Wornom, General Secretary of the Religious Education Association, who encouraged the work from the first, read and criticized an early draft of it, and is so generous as to let me quote from his report: "Your manuscript greatly appeals to me. I have found it very valuable. . . . The manuscript, as it stands, is tremendously worthwhile."

CHAPTER 1

Freedom *v.* Fear

This book is in the fortunate position of having to say only a few central things. It says first that children learning about God and faith at home and in church have the right to a completer religious literacy in and through their schools, and, if children, then also the people and the nation. It says secondly that religious literacy, somewhat hard to come by in America, is needed and is a great good. Thirdly, it makes detailed suggestions as to how this good can be achieved, partly through free and democratic American schools. It says that anybody concerned about the child and the republic must go to work with all men of good will to see how a wealthy and professedly free people can disentangle itself and begin to promote certain basic human goods.

All this seems simple enough, and it is simple. But to say these plain things to a public in part oblivious of them and in part violently opposed to them will not be easy. On some great issues such as basic education, racial integration and religious literacy, some of our people have

1

come alive and begun to be insistent, though many are still asleep and insensate. The condition may be unsatisfactory, but we are used to it, and it could be that by repetition and habit we have built up a status compounded of inhibitions, complexes and superstitions. In any case, we of today did not buy the situation. It was thrust on us, and we tend to settle for it. The circumstance need not be surprising; such things have happened to people as good as ourselves. But the effect is serious. It is almost as if we, who so often announce our freedom, had taken orders from some Kremlin or other. It is as if we had been told that certain constraining things are to be done and certain desirable things to be left undone. Fortunately, America is becoming aware of these "religion in school" issues, and we find more and more people willing to assume their share of the burden of trying to do something about them.

In this book, we are going to be reckless enough to declare for religion in the schools, and by "religion in the schools" we mean just what we say. Right through this book we mean religion in all American schools, on all levels, and in all types of schools. High and low schools, kindergarten and college, technical and liberal, schools tax-supported and schools not tax-supported (all of them, of course, as "public" as the White House or the Lincoln Memorial) Army and Navy schools, church-affiliated schools, non-denominational-religious, sectarian-religious, sectarian-irreligious, and secularist-religious schools—we mean all of them. We have had some Communist schools and perhaps have some of them now. We would mean them too if they could in any way be considered American schools.

When we say religion in the schools, we mean in and by and through the schools. Religion in and by and through homes and churches—that is taken for granted. We mean religion as a subject to be studied, not religion as a matter of indoctrination or imposed dogma, nor religion to be practiced as ritual and ceremony—unless perhaps in school dramas—nor, in public schools, religion to be practiced as any one religious body such as Catholics or Baptists or Hindus practices it. With Thomas Jefferson and Horace Mann, historically our greatest proponents of public schools, we mean religion taught as a subject in the schools and on account of the schools, and not by any means in spite of the schools. We mean religion taught in all schools objectively and scientifically, as any subject must be taught.

But even so, "reckless" is the word for anyone declaring for religion in any shape or form in American public schools. He is almost as reckless as was the Supreme Court in declaring for desegregation of public schools.

Under the wise tutelage of time and an historical evolution of legal decisions, American tax-supported schools are disallowed—that is the way we interpret the First Amendment—from putting youths through the paces of the Catholic or Baptist or Hindu way of worshipping God, or through the paces of secularist worship of gods. So much is evident to all. Yet Justice Black in his strange and alien doctrine in the McCollum decision notwithstanding, the federal government itself, in the person of every Congress and every President, has aided religion, all religion and particular religions. As Justice Douglas said in the Zorach decision, as if correcting Justice Black, the American way has always been a close tie-in between religion and government, a symbiosis quite advantageous (we would say) to each party. Through the schools or otherwise, to build up a particular religion so that in effect it would become the national and established religion, would be altogether another thing, and this is one of the things forbidden by the First Amendment.

In its public schools, the nation may not directly promote worship in the Catholic or the Baptist or the Hindu way, and it may not indoctrinate in any such religion or again in a secularist sectarian religion. It may not attempt to "make" children religious or to "keep" them religious in any particular and sectarian way.

That is one thing. It is quite another thing to teach "religion" as a given historical and existential reality. To refuse to teach it is to refuse to be objective and scientific. The refusal, besides being a sort of demonstration in dishonesty, amounts to a national vote for obscurantism. "The exclusion of religious subject matter which so largely prevails," said Dr. Johnson and the Committee on Religion and Education (for the American Council on Education), "is neither required on the grounds of public policy nor consistent with sound educational principles." * That is one of the justest declarations ever made on the subject, and we thank Dr. Johnson and the Committee for it. To keep children in enforced ignorance of what goes on in the religions of the nation and of the world is not worthy of our people and would not be worthy of a people that had even a glimmer of hope to be free and enlightened.

Today the best thing about American educators is that they are beginning to stir, and some of them are terribly exercised over real problems. All admit that the situation is urgent. Problems are legion, and everybody is talking about the schools and almost vilifying them. If anybody had dared to say pre-sputnik what everybody says now about the schools, he would have been run out of town; we were chauvinist on the subject, now we begin to be realistic. The problems are so serious that a branch of

* *The Relation of Religion to Public Education: the Basic Principles.* Washington, D.C., 1947; p. 27.

the National Educational Association names forty problem areas and sets forty groups to work on them. Forty problem areas—offhand and routine.

Here are a few of our "problem areas." 1. Now that American schools have been shown up and have to quit bragging, what are we going to do: a) about really training teachers of science? b) about basic scientific research? c) about catching students early, and then early and late really fetching them up with love for and competence in science? 2. What are we prepared, at least in good will, to do about general basic learning, in history, languages, and mathematics as well as in biology and physics? 3. On all levels, we have a lot of students pouring into schools, and schools already are too few and are understaffed: so what are we to do? 4. Will we have to get federal aid to build little red schoolhouses? 5. In which senses is federal aid likely to be a solution of school problems, and in which senses is it likely to cause serious new problems? 6. Why are not educators and citizens keeping those two questions (4 and 5) together? 7. The Pasadena troubles perhaps past, who does control and who really should control schools? 8. Is it true as alleged that "educationists" and teachers' colleges have been dictating to public schools, grade and high,* and that teachers in public schools are afraid to raise questions about the trash they must cover again and again in teacher training? 9. What are schools in New York City or elsewhere to do about delinquent children in schools, and also about the liberal needs and the vocational needs of normal teen-agers? 10. What can we do about insufficient salaries, inadequate teacher manpower, and the high cost of education? 11. The public is far from sold on us educators, on our dignity and importance, and

* Rear-Admiral Rickover (*Education and Freedom*, pp. 192-3) claims that critics of education still are censored and boycotted.

our products: what kind of ruction should we raise about that? 12. Does democracy presuppose that citizens should take as a principle "maximum education for everybody"? 13. What is democracy in education?

Evidently we are in for rough weather, and, to try to get a breath of relief, some of our educator brethren have been busy doing two non-academic and really political things: they have been ganging up to "sell the schools" to a reluctant public, and they are also busy setting up a lobby in Washington.

Though of course sympathetic to these many real problems, in this book we insist on giving high priority to the problem of religion in all American schools. Other radical problems, yes; basic education in basic things, scientific education for those who can take it, and liberal education for many and if possible for all—yes, of course. But here we are writing on another fundamental problem. We want general literacy, scientific and historical literacy, and along with them, and at the very bottom of them, we want religious literacy in teachers and students, and this we want, in part, in and through American public and private schools.

That is a major problem—religion in education. It is just possible that we in America, smart and free as we are, are not smart enough to achieve it, or not free enough: just as conceivably we are not smart enough and free enough to achieve basic education and desegregated education. Talking about those basic matters was for a long time taboo. In the three areas, nevertheless, we must go forward now with all deliberate speed, and in any event it is going to take courage and vision to begin even to think seriously about these awkward hang-over problems and how on earth they can be solved.

Over a century ago we began balking at the problem

of "religion in education." But today we have to begin all over again and try to think our way through the problem in all its complicated relations. Because of given circumstances, we the people will be forced to experiment, to feel our way, and to go at the problem piecemeal and only a step at a time. The rebuilding of worlds is not to be done in a day. Nevertheless we in this book as well as we the people must raise the question. We have reached the stage where we must break wide open this whole question, which for a long time has been heavily censored. In practice, to wrestle even locally with the problem will require prudence and patience and maturity.

At the start, and to keep people from being too much frightened, we remark that knowing God in education has at least three sides to it. One side is knowing God, simply and somehow coming to know God; and this, though it is routine for children and primitives, is, in its farthest and grandest reaches, difficult enough to exercise great minds such as Aristotle, Anselm and Spinoza. Besides, there is the question on which levels and by which methods this side of the problem should be tackled; and also how we could, at least at once, find professors with the needed sense of reverence to teach children to know God. A second side is knowing and loving God in and through education, much as we might know and love America or George Washington in and through education. We speak here of God or America or Washington as an object to be known and loved. Under this heading the problem consists in being somehow introduced to God in such a way that we would in effect, whatever of intent, be invited to love God. This side of the knowing, in which the object—whatever the object in question—becomes "connatured" to us, and we to the object, is likely to include "commitment," and of course if aimed at in public schools, would almost certainly be seen on an objective view as contrary to the First Amendment. American public schools may aim at commitment in the case of America or Washington, but may not aim at commitment in the case of God. Whether this provision in our total national life is, from an ideal point of view, a good one, we long ago chose it, and it will continue to be our choice, and is probably the only manageable way in any highly pluralistic society. The third side of the knowing, which, for some students and some professors and some schools, might be the whole, would consist in coming to know about God. This would naturally break into two parts: into knowing what it is that certain people such as Jews or Lutherans or Mohammedans or Bushmen believe they know about God, and then knowing these peoples' corresponding social orchestrations in their forms of worship.

Each of these three, *knowing God, knowing and loving God,* and *knowing about God and worship,* is rightly and radically a problem common to schools of all types and on all levels. But at least the problem of actual personal commitment, since it is always identified with some particular religion, is insoluble in public schools. When we thus make no room for commitment we know that we part company with certain pious people. Commitment must be studied in all schools, nevertheless, on the proper levels as a given social phenomenon.

Events and circumstances have pushed the study of God and religion out of schools. The effect is a resultant narrowing, and the vast majority of Americans, once they take the situation fully into account, dislike the effect. Just now we mention two of these untoward circumstances, and quite unlikely ones, at that. One is the departmentalizing of "religion" as a course taught at least in church-related schools and colleges. Our own assumption is that God and religion are somehow "there" in the study of literature and philosophy and history and anthropology. The trouble is that any such subject is itself departmentalized half to death, and God and religion are, at best, completely remanded to a shut-in specialty called "religion" or "theology." By His power and love and goodness, God (so say Christian philosophers, and Jews such as Spinoza) is present everywhere, but in schools God as a subject of study is specialized, isolated, narrowed almost to the vanishing point. When Josiah Royce was once upon a time teaching a course on "God" at Harvard, and no doubt teaching it in considerable perspective, William James said that God was sitting for His portrait by Royce. But today we get God out of focus, if at all. In Catholic schools, which are our most generally developed religious schools, God or religion as an object to be studied is, like every object of study in every school, departmentalized, a condition probably as serious in Protestant and Jewish schools. As is often remarked, in many European universities, also, the department of theology is isolated and might as well not be there at all, so far as the rest of the university is concerned. The same holds for other subjects such as philosophy and literature. Each is specialized and is engaged in scolding all others for failure to build one world of knowledge.

A second unlikely circumstance is this. We might very well expect seminaries, training clergymen and rabbis, to rescue the study of God and religion from insularity and narrowness. This they usually fail to do. For one thing, they are set up and operated for professional *ad hoc* purposes. The result is, if any such thing is possible, even less liberal than that of the departmentalized college courses in "religion." Besides, most American schooling in theology has been largely limited to apologetic and propaganda demands. This motive makes finally for barrenness. Think of the multitudes of good men whom we have heard preaching on radio all Sunday long for these thirty years: some of these men real haranguers, humorless, a few of them seemingly unbalanced. One would hesitate to call them narrow-minded, but some of them seem sterile, men of restricted vision, not especially equipped by a liberating education to see God and man and things in perspective. It is delightful to hear a preacher, as we sometimes do, who knows history or literature or psychology. Another shortcoming is that most American seminaries have always been outside the moving, growing point of theological or other knowledge; and surely this circumstance means great loss to the education of American people. In a later chapter we must return briefly to this problem of how, in what depths and heights and relevance, the clergy are being educated, since this book, dedicated to saying how American people can be educated, not only in the things of science and nature, but in the things of God and man's relation to God, must at least briefly mention the problem of how men and women are being educated in seminaries.

Our general over-all position is that we want the education that can do its part to make men free, and education in the things of God cannot be omitted from that education. That was one of the two interrelated points made by John Henry Newman's famous *Idea of a University* a century ago; he said that only the liberally educated man is educated, and that the religiously illiterate man is not liberally educated. Though Newman was concerned about what he called "the liberalism of the day," perhaps he saw farther than he knew. In our century we might state the question somewhat differently and ask: Does it well serve the person and society when, in liberal education in arts and sciences or illiberal education such as

that in engineering and in technical high schools, we skip
the study of God and man's worship-life? For the present,
we note Jefferson's reply. Jefferson said that "instruction
in religious opinion and duties" was to be included (at
the state university he was initiating in Virginia) for the
good of society.

That social aspect of the question may well be the more
important, above all in a time of world crisis. What are
we to expect as over-all social results, e.g., as regards
delinquency and political subversion, when we have left
the study of God and of worship out of education for
children and young men and women? What are Beatniks
or other youths to think of us? If in the omission we are
aiding and abetting an irreligious society, is that the kind
of society we wish to produce? What kind of society *is*
it—secularist-Communist, or secular non-Communist? Consider for a moment Toynbee's position. For the sake of
argument we may take Toynbee's study of civilization as
the greatest effort in the humanities in our time. Now
Toynbee's reply to our question, which naturally is also
his question, is unequivocal. He says that society without
religion and the God-idea is not only truncated, but historically it is non-existent. That, in even stronger terms, was
Berdyaev's reply in his study of Russian psychology and
atheistic Communism.* Berdyaev said that the idea of man
without the idea of God makes no sense at all and cannot
even be conceived; and of course Berdyaev made a great
deal of the fact that Communism has its gods and makes the
ineluctable demand that all faithful Communists worship
those gods. Primitives have gods and worship, Communists
have gods and worship, and so with both our own believers
and our own secularists. What then about an alleged basic

* Nicholas Berdyaev, in *Vital Realities*. New York, 1932.

education, a scientific education and a liberal education
with never a word about God and worship? Had we not
better think twice about which gods are going to be worshipped through our schools?

These are shocking questions and yet they are major
questions for the vast and growing educational establishment in America.

Take three of the most notable over-all products of
education as we now have it in America. First, we get a
world of practical education, all the way from typewriting
to engineering and business administration and law and
theology and medicine. Second, in spite of many weak
teachers and a poor start, some of our students eventually
have been getting an education in science; as an end-
product a vast amount of this runs to the practical and
commercial-industrial, and yet much of it is basic, "pure,"
theoretic and liberal. Third, some liberal education is certainly achieved; some of it is incidental though real, and
some is outright and consciously sought: for instance, the
study of Plato, which is carried on in many colleges and
which has to include language, literature, history and philosophy, is not primarily for practical ends, but in order
to understand Plato and to live again with him great problems and a glamorous attempt to solve them.

With so much prefaced, our business in this book may be
restated. Our business is to say that any of those end-
products, minus an introduction to the story of God and
of worship, is the result of a truncated education. A business
man, brought to the peak of business administration, is, if
he has only a pious and Sunday School introduction to the
phenomena of religion, still a poorly educated man. A
scientist, with or without liberal learning, is, if he lacks
appropriate introduction to the things of faith and God,
still an uneducated man. And a man liberally educated

in science and history, literature and philosophy, and yet immunized to the world of theological lore, is still only beginning to be liberally educated.

Such a half-education, and that is what we now achieve, means that the business man or scientist or liberal artist is trying to fly minus a wing. He is ill-adjusted to facts, to the universe, even to nature: I mean to accessible nature; and in this important regard he is really pre-primitive.

A Christian lawyer, well tutored in a famous law school, has reported: "The only time we heard the name of God was when we prayed." We are suggesting that such an education is not fair to the facts, to the young man or woman or to society. Among primitives, such an inhibition would rarely if ever occur; and in any case it easily runs into an absolutizing of the relative, and could not make sense for a citizen being educated to protect and promote justice in society.

Far from being new, the question of God and religion in education was old even in America a hundred years ago. For many generations it has been an old question in England and Ireland and France and Germany, and it remains an acute question in several countries. As Professor Marrou shows,* the question was hot in the days of Julian the Apostate, so much so that, anxious to get rid of Christians as teachers in the Empire, Julian put pressure on them and succeeded in a venture seldom credited to him: in being the occasion of the first Christian school. Christians rebelled because those of them who taught Homer and Hesiod without believing in pagan gods were to be denounced as immoral and ordered either to apostatize or to quit teaching. In Russia, likewise, the old problem of

* H. I. Marrou, *A History of Education in Antiquity*. New York, 1956; pp. 323-324.

God and religion in education, a problem thought by simple minds to have been once for all ousted, remains real. There, as Dr. Korol indicates,* children are wholly subordinated to the Revolution; in boarding schools (said *Pravda,* June 28, 1956) "the educational influence of teachers embraces the entire life of children"; and even teachers of mathematics "should realize the general goals of a communist upbringing."

Put the problem in another way. Think what it might mean to Russia and to mankind if people in Russia could be freed from total devotion to the State and could have been freed these forty years from worship of—i.e., paying the highest tribute to—Lenin, Stalin and Khrushchev. The minimum desirable thing would be for Russian youth to be allowed to see religion as a world-wide global phenomenon. But think what it might mean for us and for mankind if, along with education in practical things and in high science and in liberal arts, our own youth could have access to a common education in religious literacy.

This old question of God and religion in education has turned up and will keep turning up as the bad penny of educational theory and practice. It has kept troubling most of the great educational theorists and leaders of the past century: Newman as everybody knows, and Whitehead who was at his richest and best on this subject, and Irving Babbitt, Jacques Maritain, Christopher Dawson, and Robert M. Hutchins. Not one of these could let the problem alone. We may therefore wonder at the simplicity of people, surely not liberally educated, who, at least until sputnik, kept saying that the chief educational problems of our day are quantitative; more buildings, more teachers, more pay—as if, given loads of buildings and teachers and pay, we

* Alexander K. Korol, *Soviet Education for Science and Technology.* New York, 1957; pp. 33-34, 69-70.

would automatically achieve the freedom implied in know-ing the truth.

But how are any studies on religion and worship to get inside the door of the American public school? Is that door not barred? Put in that realistic way, the question already looks a little naive. But let us put it in another simple and justified way: Are studies on God and religion and worship to be allowed inside at all, or is the American door as tightly shut against them as the Russian door? That looks like a mere rhetorical question. The question does not meet the difficulty, which we all know is great. Look at our mighty fortress, the "separation principle." Who is so bold as to try to scale Jefferson's famous one-hundred-and-sixty-year-old "wall"? A mere iron curtain can stop information and the flow of knowledge. Think what an iron wall as solid as the Constitution can do.

We the people were innocent enough in building up this high wall, and thought we were protecting freedom, the Constitution and the American way. Dr. F. Ernest Johnson has reported that in studying the actual situation, the committee on Religion and Education found two strange at-odds situations: a) some cases of "religious activities" in schools, at variance with the McCollum decision (later, Dr. Johnson saw these as really in agreement with the Zorach decision); and b) "We found a conspicuous lack of any-thing approximating an 'American way' with respect to the relation of religion to public education. There were ev-idences of more or less deliberate avoidance of religious subject matter even when it was clearly intrinsic to the discipline concerned." *

A "conspicuous lack of anything approximating an

* F. Ernest Johnson, "Policies and Recommendations of the American Council on Education Committee on Religion and Education." *Religious Education,* v. 52 (July-Aug. 1957), p. 249.

'American way' "—this is sufficiently ominous. So too of "deliberate avoidance" of matter intrinsic to disciplines.

A study of the historical growth of this lack and this avoidance of religious subject matter could throw great light on American civilization, and it would be found that one cause for maintaining the wall, if perhaps not for building it, is fear, and another is lack of freedom. The result of the lack and avoidance can only be unbalanced and ill-educated minds.

Take parallel cases of our success in building up walls which are high and as if impregnable. Notice the strong language, the "wall" and "iron curtain" language used by Chief Justice Taney in the Dred Scott decision (1856): ". . . a perpetual barrier was intended to be erected between the white race and the one which they had reduced to slavery, and governed with absolute and despotic power." We built up quite a wall; whether it is internationally scandalous or not, it is a wall; and at last the interracial wall has turned, for many in North and South, almost into an anti-racial wall. There it is, strong as iron, and perhaps in one hundred or five hundred years it will still stand and we shall not be able to scale it. There it stands, in sight of men professing democracy. More recently, at the insistence of Russia, a mighty and unscalable wall has been building up between Communist and free nations, and that too has got to the point where it is so formidable as to keep out freedoms and knowledge.

Three strong walls, "thou shalt nevers": the white-black wall described in such terrifying words by Chief Justice Taney, the Iron Curtain wall, and a wall against teaching anything about religion in American public schools. High and mighty walls built of iron, built on rock, defying man and time to surmount them or to tear them down. The sum of what they say is that man shall not be free.

The question, however, is whether man is naturally thus unfree, or whether he has only made himself unfree. When we come to think of it, the commitment in each case is to a kind of perpetual slavery. Walls can be good or bad things. They are bad when they block freedom.

In our country, people have been almost overwhelmed with freedoms, and at last we simply take Parnell's words for granted: "No man shall set bounds . . ." * Among our freedoms we have enjoyed for the most part a sort of wide-open academic freedom. This freedom is a part of freedom of speech, and Jefferson himself said that freedom of speech (in the press) is our most precious and decisive freedom. But freedom stops dead at this "never-never" wall of "no religion in school." Our people take it literally: separation means separation and a wall means a wall. Lovers and exponents of freedom, Americans are thus left denying the very thing they affirm. They say that freedom is a fine and noble thing, a meaningful goal that they live for and are ready to die for, and undoubtedly they are sincere. But ramming into this wall, their freedom is jarred and becomes meaningless.

That road block, seemingly written into the Constitution, is a dead-end, and we must suppose that back of it are some historically good reasons. One reason is fear. At the start, of course, the fear was twofold and our forefathers had to watch both ways. They were afraid that religion itself would not be free. The other fear, also well justified, was that some one church such as the Episcopal or Presbyterian would take over and be our officially established national religion, and then the freedom of other churches

---

* I am paraphrasing Parnell's words about "the boundary of a nation." Lincoln's words would also express the American dream: "I intend no modification of my oft-quoted wish that all men everywhere could be free."

and their adherents would be reduced and perhaps destroyed; to tell the simple truth, many Protestants in our early history wanted union of state and Protestant church, and the records show that they had it. When the break came officially in 1833 between church and state in Massachusetts, Henry Ward Beecher's father, a deeply religious man, wept as if it were the end of the world. Americans had and they still have something real to fear. In our historical background this "something real to fear" has become so habitual with Jews and Catholics that they are attuned to it and thrive on it. Even today a hang-over from that feeling still counts heavily with some Protestant minds: the feeling that we have in a quasi-unofficial way a union of America and Protestantism.

Generalized, what we fear far down, though not yet at bottom, is the old church-state problem, not union or disunion of church and state, but just that persistent and bothersome problem of one jamming the other. Church and state always keep clashing, a problem to which we shall return in another context. It is a question of degree, but in a Jewish society, or a Christian one or a Jewish-Christian-secularist one, church and state intermittently do clash, and it appears that if the two coexist they will continue to clash. Our common attempt at a solution is simple: don't let the two meet at all, don't let them move in the same orbit. If they never meet they will never collide. Therefore keep them in air-tight "separate" worlds, neither church nor state having anything to do with the other.

Is that what we really and radically mean? Do we mean an impossible thing like that? Are we simple enough to suppose such a thing? Or do we only mean that each, church and state, should be free and independent and itself?

If that is what we mean, we are only for a distinction, not a separation. But at that the central practical question of this book remains. It can now be stated intelligibly and defensibly, but it is still a question. If we are to keep church or religion in one corner and state or politics in its distinct though not "separated" corner, how can our people, with a conglomeration of religious faiths, find freedom to have studies of God and religion in all the schools of America? Do we really have *this* freedom?

The fear which Americans experienced at the beginning is, even today, a standing and justified fear. It is the reasonable fear, based on known instances of such an eventuality, that some one religion will gobble up political power; and though we have no present fear of political leaders crippling religion in America, all know that in many nations political leaders have done that kind of thing, and they keep doing it. But our fears have another and quite different basis. Most of our fear historically has been based on the fact that a dominant religious majority always tends to throw its political and non-political weight around, and as a rule without the slightest idea of what it is doing. In our country this body is obviously the Protestant body, elsewhere it is Catholic, or Hindu, or Moslem. The dominant body tends to get a finger in the political pie and to keep others shoved off; it tends to cow minority religious groups and keep them in an inferior and relatively unfree position. Others simply do not have in school or society the effective privileges and freedoms that the big religious majority has. Just this kind of thing happens in many vital phases of other matters such as the racial problem. In the barest technical and official sense the Negro, even in the South, has the same basic rights as the white. But let us see him obtain and exercise those basic rights! The dominant majority effectively if perhaps unofficially sees to it that the Negro does not exercise his natural rights and freedoms.

Take a more nearly parallel situation. Officially the Irish Free State has no established church. But it would be remarkable if the strong Catholic majority never made it tough, socially and really, though unofficially, tough, on religious minorities, and also if the religious majority did not at any time or in any way meddle in politics. Pressure in regard to censorship might be a case in point. In the United States, officially without a state religion, Catholics and Jews have always experienced strong religious-political pressures and discrimination. Evidence of this discrimination was far too clear when in 1958 a top man of Protestants and Other Americans United for Separation of Church and State broke publicly from that interesting group with the declaration that it denied to Catholics the freedoms it assumed for Protestants. He said that, according to the POAU, a Catholic candidate for office in America needs to be given the once-over by this censor group, whereas so far as a Protestant candidate in the same country is concerned we must let his theological-political opinions go scot-free under cover of his Protestantism; i.e., under the assumed union of America and the Protestant church. Likewise, the Fair Campaign Committee * said, under release of September 14, 1959: "'58 Election Smear Doubled '56, Catholics top religious target."

This feeling of discrimination must be normally expected. It breaks out when a Catholic runs for office or is appointed to office, and it sometimes breaks out in unlikely places. When President Eisenhower appointed a Catholic to the Supreme Court in 1956, the same feeling of discrimination reappeared; it had appeared, for instance, when the out-

---

* Fair Campaign Committee, 8 East 66th Street, N.Y.C., 21.

standing Roger Taney, a Catholic, was appointed to the
Court in 1836. In 1956, the National Liberty League of
New York, said to be "devoted to the separation of church
and state," rose up on its hind legs and practically demanded that the appointee to the Court take a special
oath to the League. A Senate committee, whose duty it
was to review the appointment, took a different view.
Senator Kefauver's report for the committee was this:

> I said the very basis of our country is that one's religion
> and politics and thoughts are free . . . I said I hoped the
> public would not feel that this is the kind of issue which
> we think has any relevance at all. The entire committee
> agreed with that statement.

It is an excellent thing to have racial and religious freedoms protected officially by the Irish or the English or the
American Constitution. It may be quite another thing to
be actually and all the time blest with those freedoms.

At this point, we reach the bottom reason for fear. People are afraid of each other. Having suffered discrimination,
Jews are vigilantly and all the time afraid of Christians,
and Jews and Catholics in America are afraid of Protestants;
and seeing the growth of the Catholic population and
Catholic schools, many Protestants—as Will Herberg has
remarked—instinctively fear the loss of their own hegemony.
Many Jews are afraid to declare themselves in school as
definitely Jewish; if they do, their chances are slimmer
for getting on, for instance, in medical schools or in hospi-
tals or in employment. Protestants see what they can only
take to be discrimination in predominantly Catholic countries such as Spain; and in English-speaking countries,
Catholics for centuries knew what it meant to suffer. *

* These matters are well stated in Leo Pfeffer, *Creeds in Competi-
tion*. New York: Harper, 1958.

So we are all wary. We are all naturally afraid of each other, and given that distrustful feeling, which has become as if congenital to us, we are afraid to allow freedom to teach even one word concerning religion in American public schools on the lower levels. It is easier to say that such teaching would be unconstitutional and against "separation" than to think matters through and live matters through, and to admit that we are too scared to be effectively free.

It would be novel, and inspiring, too, if any one group were to begin to learn, in school or in church, what any other group really believes. Yet a major claim of this book is that it would be enlarging and freeing, as well as enlightening, and that as we mature and become more capable of freedom, it will be possible and feasible, and eventually we will begin to insist on providing for this normal human good.

Then we will begin to be able to wrestle like a nation of free men with the question of religion in education. Today we are almost completely stalled. That is so true that some of the best known philosophers of education are able to offer us only a little drivel on the problem. Dr. Rugg's voluminous work * on "foundations" seems not to say one word on the problem, and Dr. Brameld, writing philosophies of education in "perspective," gives us a few trivial lines † and seems never to have entered into the problem. For our part we cannot think the question is to be passed over in silence or passed over with a dozen routine words, and we are bound to see such works as thin in terms of actual knowledge as well as tame in the line

* Harold Rugg, *Foundations For American Education*. World Book Co., 1947.

† Theodore Brameld, *Philosophies of Education in Cultural Perspective*. New York: Dryden Press, 1955; p. 13.

of imagination. Where have the authors been living these forty years?

That brings us really and truly to the practical question. It is above all a question of freedom. Perhaps the study of God and religion in all the schools would be a good thing. If it should prove practicable at all, perhaps a modicum of the worship of God in schools would also be a good thing; e.g., by intervals of silent Quakerish prayer. The question first and last is whether American public and private schools are free enough and broad-based enough to have any such study, regardless of the worship. Probably we do not yet have the freedom, or just do not yet have imagination and intelligence sufficiently developed to see the way to do good things. Immaturity may be part of the problem. Of course, if a lack of freedom or intelligence or maturity is the case, we would be embarrassed to say so, even to ourselves. In that event, in and through the schools we would be free only to worship secularist gods. It would be as if some sort of high inquisitional secularist mandate had decreed that our freedom and intelligence should be stopped and be forced to be inoperative in certain matters, that certain fields of knowledge should be closed and that the mention of particular realities should be hushed up. Americans then would be lining up with Russians.

That is a possible reading of the situation. Still, we are a resourceful people, tough and resilient, so full of youthful ardor and innocence that we are unlikely to be bluffed once for all out of the path to the chief human goods. In spite of the fact that people like easy solutions, in the present matter we are almost sure, sooner or later, to break out and to dare to take the hard road to freedom.

To repeat, it is as if we had long ago got ourselves hedged in, as we did on the racial problem: and on the latter problem not a soul can doubt today that we notably lost freedom to do what needs to be done. Of course, it must be fully expected that in a society as markedly pluralistic as ours, it is and must remain difficult to have Caesar and God in the same classroom, a fact which we will have reason to repeat. The easy answer is to put God out. That procedure, however, only looks easy and is no more a solution that it would be to put Caesar out: out goes the flag, out go Washington and Jefferson and Lincoln, out go the Revolution and the record of our struggles for freedom and the whole story of history. That is far too easy a solution—putting one or the other out.

Besides, Caesar and God are not the only objects of study and devotion that sometimes seem to get in each other's way and to be poles apart. As we know too well, in both society and schools Caesar and the human person are perpetually competing for places: in England and America and more evidently in Fascist and Communist kingdoms. What are we to do, then? Are we going to disqualify Caesar and get rid of the problem, or shall we go along with Russia and declare for a radical reduction of freedoms and for all kinds of indignities to the human person?

Evidently there is only one answer. The answer is maturity and intelligent hard work, along with vigilance. The Greeks said that good and lovely things are difficult. These particular good and lovely things will continue to be difficult, the integration in the same school of colored and white, of God and Caesar. Or must we fold up and say that segregation is in each case the last word?

Among the many problems, then, in American and Western education is this terribly troublesome problem of God and worship in education, a problem that runs from kindergarten through every Yale and Harvard. If the birth rate holds up and the economy can hold its own, and of course if wars hold off, we will have more and more youths "in college." People are predicting that by 1970 we will have more than twice as many as today in college, say a jump from three to six millions. To all who have profound respect for the person and love for the social good this "going to college" must mean more, in its final product, than bigger salaries and a chance at the "quick buck" for the beneficiaries, and something more for the nation than trying desperately to keep up with sputnik. Excellent scientific studies and practical studies and liberal studies must remain inadequate so long as studies of God and religion are excluded.

From many directions events are converging to suggest that American people want a change and are hungry for the study of religion in education. Among other events, we have the phenomenon of religion showing a notable pick-up, at least in church-going and church building, if conceivably not always in a corresponding spirit of humility and sacrifice in believers. At a minimum, people are in effect saying that it is unsatisfactory to secularize their lives and their children's lives. Take more directly relevant matters. The regents of education in New York State began in 1951 recommending—since then they have repeatedly recommended—that each school day in the public schools of the state begin by joining to the salute to the Flag "this act of reverence to God: 'Almighty God, we acknowledge our dependence upon Thee, and we beg Thy blessings upon us, our parents, our teachers and our Country.'" They recommend further that specific programs might be included

stressing the moral and spiritual heritage which is America's, the trust which our pioneering ancestors placed in

Almighty God, their gratitude to Him from Whom they freely and frequently acknowledged came their blessings and their freedom and their abiding belief in the free way of life and in the universal brotherhood of man based upon their acknowledgement of the fatherhood of their Creator, Almighty God, Whom they loved and reverenced in diverse ways. . . .

Those regents, who themselves are in this regard pioneers, have later urged that children in New York State sing "America"—"Our Fathers' God, to Thee, Author of liberty"—and that youths in that state be given a chance, we might say, *be given the freedom,* to see the documents in our history affirming God and human rights. Some objectors then said, "No, don't let children sing those songs and read those books: such things are divisive, and the separation principle debars them." Unfortunately, to debar in this case is to debar American history. We are convinced that the words "divisive" and "separation" were cover-up words and that the objectors were grinding unpatriotic axes.

Let us return quickly to the positive side. Relatively few professors in American colleges and universities have balked in line with the recalcitrant New York City group just now paraphrased. It is true that most professors have seemingly been oblivious of the "religion in education" problem, and some few have been belligerent secularists and fewer still have been Communist secularists. As a rule, the higher learning has been unafraid of the true story of American history. Americans were rather pleased than shocked when, several years ago, a new president of Harvard announced that the study of God and religion, for some time notably slighted at that school, was going to be emphasized, or when a major foundation shelled out money to help the cause along, saying that nothing could be more important for education in America. Luther Weigle, ex-dean of Yale divinity school, has claimed, though perhaps too optimistically, that what he calls the drive to secularize public schools has been "considerately blunted, if not stopped." Beginning with World War II, we have also noticed that American academic associations at the summit have been more open to ideas on God and on natural law (long mistakenly supposed to be merely a religious matter and an affirmation by Catholics only) than they had for a long time been. The American Philosophical Association is now turning over whole sessions to discussions on God and on natural law, something it did not do and was not free to do a generation ago. Anthropologists such as Kluckhohn and the late Dr. Ralph Linton have swung over, also, to affirm at least what they call ethical universals and pan-human universals, a new affirmation for men in that field. Kluckhohn even speaks of discovering "inevitabilities." In passing we note that there is plenty of evidence that both the philosophers of law and morals and the anthropologists have been scared out of a facile positivism by totalitarian powers.*

Consider another indication of the national concern for religion in public schools. As is well known, the National Conference of Christians and Jews has existed since 1928 and precisely on account of the terrible politico-religious scandals of the 1928 elections and has operated to encourage members of one faith to understand and respect members of other faiths. A natural trouble-shooter, the Conference started all over again in the winter of 1957-1958

---

* See, e.g., Clyde Kluckhohn, "Ethical Relativity: *Sic et Non*," *Journal of Philosophy*, 52 (Nov. 10, 1955), 663ff. "I think we must admit the abandonment of the doctrine of untrammelled relativity is a reaction to the observation of social consequences."

to work nationally and in many local centers to consider the problem of the study of religion in American public schools, and the freedom or non-freedom of education in religion in those schools. The conference has collected materials for such a study and is prepared to promote discussion of the tangled problems.*

We already noted that the same National Conference (NCCJ) gave the first push to serious and competent studies on the subject of religion in education, studies made by the American Council on Education. In 1939, studies were made and conferences held by the NCCJ "to clarify the issues." The American Council on Education published the report and then, taking over the work of continuing the studies, formed an official national Committee on Religion and Education. Still in operation, this Committee has written the two reports from which we have quoted: a) in 1947, *The Relation of Religion to Public Education: the Basic Principles,* and b) in 1953, *The Function of the Public Schools in Dealing with Religion.†*

The former document said (pp.vi, 31): ". . . if untenable proposals are here and there advanced and adopted in the field of religious education, they may be in fact a result of an educational policy that has tended to isolate religion from other phases of community life. Nothing elemental in human life can be indefinitely isolated . . . In the study of the various phases of community life—govern-

* The Conference is promoting acquaintance with these pamphlets among others: "Religion and the Public Schools" by Joint Advisory Committee of the Synagogue Council of America and the NCRA Council (9 E. 38 St., NYC 16, 1956), and "The Church and the Public Schools" (Board of Christian Education, Presbyterian Church in the U.S.A., Witherspoon Bldg., Philadelphia, 1957; price, fifteen cents).

† Both are published by the American Council on Education, Washington, D.C.

ment, markets, industry, labor, welfare, and the like—there would seem to be no tenable reason for the omission of contemporary religious institutions and practices."

The second study said, in part (p.71): ". . . many leaders in all sections and in most communities think that the present state of affairs with respect to religion and public education is not satisfactory and that the problem should be studied until a satisfactory solution is found."

These several bits of evidence adduced by us may be straws indicating only a breeze. But in any case many of the people as well as many scholars are dissatisfied with the situation and some stir is being made. More will be said and done, and lively pro and con feelings will be aroused. The problem is long-standing and is deep and difficult. It is a social, psychological, and moral problem as well as religious and educational. At a minimum we may say this: all understand now when it is said that "religion out of education" perfectly expresses the Russian ideal, but neither the historical nor the present American ideal. In practice, of course, the facts might compel us to be ironic and to put the matter in another way, as follows. Perhaps Russians have surpassed us in basic education and in science and mathematics. But here is the hitch: do we perhaps keep up with them in ousting God and religion from the whole of education?

Happy to have the promise and beginning of assurances from both the people and the scholars, we proceed now to study the entire question of religious literacy in American schools. This means that we shall have to study it from every angle and in a dozen contexts. The situation within which we do this is sufficiently urgent. A good pessimist would be in all his glory, with the world crisis and our own moral crises among adults, and among child

delinquents, some of them operating in schools. If therefore religion in the schools, along with that in homes and
churches, is any good, let us by all means have it. Dr.
John Meyers, then chancellor of the New York State board
of regents, a few years ago put this side of things strongly *:

> To fill the ranks of scientists, teachers, statesmen, en-
> gineers and givers of the law, with men and women, no
> matter how skilled, who do not possess minds disciplined
> by recognition of those things basically good and those
> things despicably evil, is to invite disaster. In this age,
> the need for renewed emphasis on moral and spiritual
> truths, on faith in God and in country, is critically ur-
> gent.

Meyers was right in saying that the situation is urgent.
Even so, we are aware that a person is taking his life in
his hands by daring to say a word about the supposedly
buried question of "religion in the schools." He will be
declared a public nuisance, and no doubt justly, too, and
will be thought a disturber of a hard-earned peace. He will
be challenged to square his pet ideas with a barrage of
questions—about the "separation" principle, about public
schools as a *sine qua non* for democracy, about "public"
tax money used, as it is in some places, for the welfare
of "private" school children, about moral and spiritual values in the schools, about freedom to conduct and attend
private schools, about freedom to teach religion as a part
of the first freedom, about released time on and off the
premises, and about the right to religious literacy itself.
And finally, within the over-all question, he must be willing
to face a pair of questions which we ourselves take to be
fundamental. First, outside the theological field, is there

* See *New York Times*, Nov. 17, 1954.

any actual or possible learning that may justifiably be called Judeo-Christian learning? That is a bothersome question, and we shall see that many Christian educators, sometimes for strategic reasons and sometimes for historical reasons, are afraid to deal with it. The other question is the practical one of whether, given our freedoms and lack of freedoms, anything after all can be done.

The fix that we the people are in is this. Our old car is stalled. Can we get it going again, and if not, what would it take to buy a new car? Is a man a heretic because he asks these questions? Heretic or no heretic, this writer goes on record as saying that a forced secularism in schools is in restraint of freedom and is a violation of the Constitution. Does anyone want to take the other side?

CHAPTER 2

The Right to Religious Literacy

A basic thesis in this book is that every man has the right to religious literacy. He has this right in two senses. As by nature he is free, he should be left free to know—to know about things and to know things, to know about God and to know God. Secondly, he has a right to be enabled by his education—and a Sunday School education falls short of it—to read whatever is readily legible as regards God in nature and history. Nature has not done man out of the right to know God; anthropology and history invite him to exercise that right; and neither society in general nor an educational system in particular should ask him to forfeit the right.

The statement of our thesis may be yet stronger. The child should not be hindered, his mind should not be hobbled by ignorance or indoctrination, whether left as a negative precipitate of schools or of the larger society.

As person and citizen, man has a right to certain fundamental goods of body and mind and freedom. He cannot fully be a person unless he has ready access to these goods, and the most radical and native demand in him is that he be genuinely a person.

Man naturally wants to know, and it is good for him to know. That, so far, is his nature and his good. It is good for him to know God, to know nature, to know the mind of man with all its achievements and possibilities, to know man's love-power with its vast possibilities, and to know that each of these possibilities, in the life of mind and of love, has quasi-infinite dimensions.

Youths like to observe the antics of toads and caterpillars and kittens, to know all about the conquering of outer space, the climbing of mountains, and making of touch-downs, about great mysterious physical things right at our door, such as atoms and satellites. In its own nature, know-ing is a spiritual event, and the story of man's knowledge and freedom, though we are used to it, is a thriller. By intelligence and freedom man conquers Everest and the moon and progressively finds the atom stammering the secrets of the universe, so that science, though ordinarily dealing with matter, is first of all a spiritual achievement. Think of what man's spirit is able to do even without equip-ment and precision instruments. Think of what Homer, after all a man, did in merely one passage: when he de-scribed the design wrought by Hephaestus, a blacksmith god, on the shield of Achilles. Think of St. Francis so easily seeing the heavenly-father dimension in sun and wolf and fish, of Columbus finding new worlds, of Lincoln striving to free man.

The child should know about these things, and should know these things. He has "a right to." He too is made for greatness. This quintessence of dust! A little less than the angels! Man is so great that God is mindful of him.

Children should know about and should know these things.

Of course, man is perpetually stopped by mystery, and himself is an enigma and mystery. But, over and over stopped before the mystery of life and time and being, man can know that he has encountered mystery, and fairly dumb as he is before some great and near things—life, sense knowledge, intellectual knowledge, freedom, and ultimate meaning—he can know that some day he may be able to make any of these declare themselves. His job is to try to conquer the unconquerable, and at times he succeeds. He is able to grasp something of what Job says: "Lo, these things are said in part of His ways: and seeing we have heard scarce a little drop of His word, who shall be able to behold the thunder of His greatness?" There are greater things in heaven and on earth and in outer space than are dreamt of in the complacent "bourgeois" philosophy which so long thrived on its own ignorance. These truths too, a child, once he has reached the high-school level, should begin to know.

Man can know man, even though the greatness and meaning of man will continue to be inexhaustible. He can know that perhaps new Einsteins, new Darwins, new Augustines and Aristotles may some day unseal some of the old tombs.

It is reasonable to become ecstatic about these things and to join Swinburne in singing a song to man. We are affirming them merely as a buildup for saying that it would be intolerable if the student did not have the freedom and the introductory bit of enablement to know man, even the encouragement and invitation to know man: the external man of anthropology and history, of psychology and philosophy, and of art and literature, and the man of intimate personal experience—"the warmth and intimacy of the contemplated me." * It is important to keep the gates open if we want to defend and promote democracy and if we pretend to believe at all in man.

So too about the child's coming to know God along with knowing nature and man. The child has the right to know the reality and depth and glamor of the whole world. "No man has the right to set bounds . . ."

Our first suggestion comes to a very simple one. It is bad for the child not to know man, nature and God. It is an evil thing, which means a cross-grained condition leaving man hurt and cheated, maimed in his being and only half human; and in this regard think how man historically has been cheated and is now cheated! Our assumption, which is the assumption of every educator under the sun, is that man, able to know, is made to know. Of course because of the kind of being he is and the kind of world he inhabits, he also needs to know. Knowing satisfies an interest and meets a vital need. But in the first place, man naturally wants to know. Left ignorant, he is like a cripple or a blind man; he is thereby deflated in dignity, and far short of par for man.

Man is made to know as the bird to fly. It is an evil thing for the bird not to be able to fly and not to be allowed to fly. He is hardly living a bird-life at all. The bird is reduced in stature, short-changed in his natural existence, and has not a chance to be what the bird presently and actually is and what the bird in his nature demands to be. Tough on the bird—he is not allowed to be.

It is the same with the child. Nature is generous toward the child, and also stepmotherly. The child is a king in potency, but is checked and held up; he is the royal heir, and at the same time a sort of starveling and orphan. He can in time come into his own, but does not necessarily

* Words of William James.

do it. His arriving depends above all on "education," which in a broad sense includes far more than "schools." * So the educators have always supposed—the child is to know. The starveling orphan wanting to be and ready to be the royal man-heir and waiting for the chance to be just that—such is the central doctrine which in spite of a pragmatic immediacy keeps trying to break out in Dewey's compendious *Democracy and Education,* and it is central in Jacques Maritain's extremely compact *Education at the Crossroads,* where Maritain begins by citing the famous words of Pindar that our chief duty, in education and out of it, consists in becoming who we are; i.e., in becoming man. The same idea is central in the theory and practice of any who at any time deserve to be called educators.

Another way to say this is to say that genuine educators always presuppose "nature" and "teleology." They believe that man has a particular "nature" and believe that nature in man is a tendency or drive toward fulfilment. That is, nature in man has a drive toward ends. This tending is integral to man's being and is autonomous, though in a Tsarist or Communist kingdom the attempt is to drive man contrary to nature. Which simply means that in such a kingdom, man's freedom and autonomy, given as part of his being, is disrespected.

Before proceeding with our thesis on the right of children to know God in and through any American public or private school, and not merely in spite of these schools, we shall emphasize the point that man has some natural rights. This we do for two closely related reasons. First is the obvious existential reason that man in his freedom

---

* *Schools and the Means of Education* by Willis D. Nutting (Notre Dame, Ind.: Fides, 1959), a strong if sometimes cranky book, details some of the "means" other than schools.

and autonomy has suffered severe setbacks in this century. The other is that legal and moral positivism denies natural rights, and this philosophy, ruling for instance in Germany long before Hitler and popular now for some time with philosophers in America, always plays into the hands of totalitarian dictators.

For a moment consider the positivist theory. The retired German and American professor, Hans Kelsen, says that "natural law" is merely what society at any time and place decrees. The German scholar, the late Gustav Radbruch, seems to have thought so, too, but, faced by the fact of Hitler and Nazism, he discovered where believers in man must stand and he finally expressed a powerful anti-positivist view. After the Second World War, Radbruch said: "The legal positivism that ruled unchallenged among German legal scholars for decades and taught that 'law is law,' —this view was helpless when confronted with lawlessness in a statutory form. For the adherents of this view any statute, however unjust, had to be treated as law."

On the positivist view, man has no rights by nature, no freedoms, no values. Man has the "rights" and "freedoms" and "values" that society allows him, exactly those and none other. And society turns out at times to be ruled by Nazis and Communists.

In the eyes of positivism, Viennese or American, the child has the right to know God, in or out of schools, if society says he has that right. We mention this view, then, for three reasons: because it falls into the totalitarian trap, because some of our own influential philosophers in several universities go along with it, and also because anyone believing in man's rights and freedoms must repudiate such a view. In passing we note that the reaction against the positivist view has been strong. Precisely because this view matched the action of Hitler and Stalin, men of such

widely different backgrounds as the Deweyite and prag-
matist, Lon Fuller of Harvard Law School, and the Aris-
totelian realist, John Wild of Harvard University, have
declared against positivism.*

"Rights" are moral claims to be, or to have or to do something, and what we properly call human dignity and freedom is inexpressible once we delete natural human rights.
These human rights go with human being. If our friend
the bird had natural rights, he would have rights which
would exactly match his being, and he would have them,
not because they were granted to him by society or by
some wonderful democratic or autocratic ruler, but just
because of his own being in the line and species of bird.
He would not have human rights or divine rights, but "bird
rights" because of his nature as bird.

A child has rights which he cannot enforce and enjoy;
for example, the right to love and respect and to be treated
as a human being. The reason for this inability is obvious.
The same inability attaches to many adults, for example
to men in concentration camps.

Let us repeat the position. The totalitarian mind can
never grant that man has some rights because he is man.
To be a democrat is to believe in man and to believe with
Hungarian youth and all lovers of freedom that man has
some rights even though dictators should build walls to
the sky against everything human; it is to be willing to die
saying that man has some rights because he is man, and
not because he is white or colored or because he lives
in Tibet or out of Tibet.

Being a man is something more radical and important

*The reaction against positivism and for natural law is the chief
post-Hitler event in legal and ethical theory. See Leo R. Ward, "The
Natural Law Rebound," *The Review of Politics*, XXI (Jan. 1959),
pp. 114-130.

than being a citizen, or an American or a Chinaman. Being
a man means being a person, a being endowed by nature
with a certain dignity, with freedoms that may not be
touched by any political community, such as freedoms of
belief and conscience. We shall often repeat the immortal
formula of Aquinas: "Man is not subordinate in all that
he is to any political community." Not by nature, though
often in fact: race, creed, previous condition of servitude—
these are the chief factual blocks to man's freedoms and
rights.

Happily, the main Western declarations for man and
freedom have, especially during the last three centuries,
insisted on saying these things. Being a man means being
endowed by nature with an inviolable interiority, an inner
sanctum which sometimes is invaded by torturers, but
which should never be invaded. It means possessing oneself
and not being possessed as slave or as anyone's serf or
"man." It means the power to think and to act freely, and,
not less important, to win freedom by giving oneself freely
to the good of persons. It means the power to assimilate
the meaning of things, to appreciate persons and things,
to inhabit all actual and all possible worlds.

That is something of what is meant by saying that we
believe in man and his rights and freedom.

Even the poorest person, thus endowed with rights, is
by nature ambitious and is made to be a world conqueror.
By knowledge and love he can grasp the truth and being
and good of heaven and earth. All belongs to him. Is it
not the glamorous St. John of the Cross who says that all
things are mine—the stars, the streams, the world of men,
and saints and angels and their Queen, and God himself?

With intellect and will, man—evidently as wretched and
miserable as Pascal or Sartre ever made him, and evidently
a material being—is a spiritual being and a person; and in

precisely these ways, as person, as free and as knowing intellectually, he is notably like the Divine Persons. Hence again the dignity of man. He *belongs*—he is within the family of persons and is a member of that distinguished family, and this is so not by sufferance, as if by the king's condescension, but by nature. And in the whole community of the world, divine, angelic, human and sub-human, no type of being known to us is higher than the type called person.

A person is relatively out of this world, and though he is a part of nature, he is also independent of nature. He is transcendent to time and place, even though plainly immanent in them. A person, said D'Arcy in his *Mirage and Truth,* "is self-determining and can even impose his will on the world. This is the reason that man has maintained a proud spirit throughout his history and gone from success to success in exploration and in the subjugation of nature, in the advance of science and development of social relations." This fragile person, so much like the Divine Spirit, can know and command material creation. He elevates and redeems all that is beneath him. As Maritain has said, St. Francis of Assisi understood that material nature, before being exploited by industry for our use, demands to be familiarized by our love; that is to say, in loving things and the being in them, man should rather draw things up to the human level than let the machine and the desire for money reduce humanity to their measure.

This human person of whom we are making so much has rights, among which is the right to at least that modicum of knowledge enabling him to live worthy of his status as a human being. It is for the sake of him and his rights that we have schools and other freedom-making institutions. As a person, he has a natural right to at least enough knowledge to enable him to live as a person and develop as a person. What we call "a right" is a moral claim attaching to his status, his dignity, his person. Nevertheless, a moral claim is not always an enforceable claim; something gets in the way, some man, some institution or the man's own shortcomings, his ignorance, superstitions and evil habits. The thing getting in the way then fulfills the meaning of evil—something blocking nature's demand, since evil (Whitehead said, really following Aristotle) means things at cross-purposes.

Within man as person is a demand, given by nature, to live as a person, and nature has given him the ability to acquire the knowledge needed so that he can live on this highest level. If he has the ability, the need and duty to live as a person, he also has a right to the knowledge needed to accomplish the duty and really to live as a man. That evidently is putting the case at a minimum. In certain historical times, as in modern democratic society, more knowledge is needed in order to live worthily as a person and citizen. Also because of access to scientific knowledge and because of easy communications, more knowledge is readily available. In such circumstances the normal person has a right to more and the duty to seek more than that first minimum of knowledge.

In any normal instance, man has the ability to get knowledge of some basic realities. By nature he wants to do so, and we have been repeating that he needs to do so. Getting knowledge is "natural," and is more than satisfying a cooked-up "interest." I say then that man has a right to knowledge, meaning that his nature demands it, if he is really to have a chance to come through as a human being. And nature is demanding this radical and simple thing: that he at least struggle to come through. Without the possession and exercise of some rights, the rights to existence, to physical integrity, to basic freedoms, to some knowledge and to life in society, man cannot operate as a person, and nature is eternally asking him to operate as a person. This holds whether he is savage or civilized.

On occasions such as local or world-wide crises, the exercise of almost any of these rights may justly and duly be restricted. The restriction, too, is in the name of man's rights, and is a good thing. But that does not mean that even a poor and moronic man therefore possesses no rights.

Now for the present application of these simple ideas. Grant that man the person has a quasi-infinite dimension in knowing and also in spontaneously and radically giving himself to the good of the family of persons. Think what an unjust and inhuman thing we would be doing in education at home, at church and at school if we did not let children come to know about this radical generosity which is possible for them and the exercise of which is so good for them and others. How wrong it would be if we would, as we have often done during the last two or three centuries, effectively shut the child up in the dungeon of his single individual self, in a doctrine and practice of an atomistic, individual self-seeking, of every man for himself, thus not only barring children from truth, but walling them up in error—and on a matter so important for their whole life and the life of mankind. One truth that we ought to give children a chance to learn is that man is supposed to be integrated with the community, loving it and loved by it. Our general point, simply, is that children have a right to know the truth.

Take a second example. The child has a right to know that, in spite of human weakness and evil-doing, man is essentially good. If that is the nature of man, it is a shameful thing to teach, as much Western thought under some false leads has long taught, that man is essentially "corrupt." If the child followed that teaching, he would grow up to be exactly what we and nature do not want him to be—suspicious, hopelessly pessimistic, defeated and defeatist, a man-hater, and he would likely turn into the nihilist whom we deprecate. Who could be asked to respect, to love, honor and obey, and on due occasion die for, man alleged to be essentially corrupt? Fortunately, few people take seriously such a perverted doctrine.

The child has the right to know the grandeur and the possible generosity of man and the goodness of man. We must also give the child the opportunity—it's easy!—to see that man has his difficulties—is perilously situated, as Existentialists remark—is blind and weak and full of phobias.

In matters more obviously academic, it would be wrong and against the child's rights if, in our time and place, he were to be cheated in the following matters: if he received no fitting introduction to the recorded history of man, no introduction to literature or music or to man's struggles for freedom, and in general to man's achievement. That would mean no proper introduction to man as today knowable. The child would be starved, and the nation would be starved. With books and gadgets at our disposal, with the child's natural ability, his burning curiosity (as Dewey so well said) and his hunger for knowledge, and with years of schooling, we have not the right to starve the child or the nation in any of these respects.

People should not try to fool themselves. Certain disciplines such as mathematics, languages and history have proved their worth in education. Run-of-the-mine movies and TV shows can help, but learning to know nature through science and to know man through history and many studies, remains an arduous process, a long hard road demanding work and asceticism. It means hard work. Cheap shortcuts should be suspect, and infantile and soft-

touch philosophies such as "life adjustment" and condition-
ing for group life leave us far from the goal of understanding.* Happily, Dr. Conant's study of the high school,
though a little on the Pollyanna side, says just these things,
and Dr. Arthur Bestor and the Council for Basic Education
have long been saying them. The Council for Basic
Education has for some years been declaring as its statement of purpose: "That all students without exception
receive adequate instruction in the basic intellectual disciplines, especially English, mathematics, science, history
and foreign languages." The Council was at first bucked,
notably by entrenched interests, but by this time all must
agree with its obvious realism and good sense.

Whatever the means and techniques used, the child has
the right to know. It would be unforgivable if we did not
give every normal American child the chance to see the
brilliance of Russian genius which, much as we may dislike
the fact, in recent generations has probably been the greatest when we consider in combination its products in music,
literature, science, and unscrupulous statecraft; of Italian
genius which, taken in many fields and over a period of
twenty centuries (allowing it to have roots in the Romans)
is, all in all, the greatest in the Occident; of Chinese genius
which was advanced before the Roman was born. We must
let people know. In our crucial times, it would be catastrophic if, as peoples are so fond of doing, we were to beat
the drums and wave the flag so that the child would be
misled and take it for granted that ours is the wisest of
all nations, the most progressive, the leader in science and
art and education, tops in the history of man. "We," said
William Vogt, "even we fortunate Americans!" That is
the great peril for the child and for mankind. Narrowness,

* See Leo R. Ward, "The Key to Education." *The Commonweal*,
54 (July 1, 1951) pp. 183-185.

inhibitions, inflated nationalism—these are dubious roads to the great goods to which the child has a right in education. The child deserves something freer and better.

To take another central example, the child has the right to see the beauty of nature, to come contemplatively into the presence of nature's magnitude in mountains and seas and planets, her delicacy in pigeons and turtles and magnolias and in the light at sunset of a June day. The child has the ability to develop an appreciation of beauty in both nature and art, and neither the parent nor the school nor advertising on TV has the right to keep raucous and horrendous things pounding hour after hour on the child's senses and mind.

Again, take the world perpetually and progessively opening up in biology and physics and astrophysics. Today the child even in kindergarten has the right to enter, if only by a tiny first step, into that world. In our country, it is wrong for us to have at this late day poorly prepared teachers of science, and it would be wrong for pusillanimous teachers of teachers in one way or another to hold back the curious mind of the child and thus to jockey the child out of a minor introduction to science, the most assured and exhilarating modern achievement. Everything should be done to encourage the child to begin to see how nature works. Several companies have brought out good, graded books on science for school children. Besides these, we need to keep littered around, at school and at home, cheap paperbacks on science for children and pamphlets, too, and leaflets. We need twenty-five-cent paperbacks on astronomy, geology and biology. To tell the truth, we cannot find anything like them, and a publisher has suggested that the graded textbooks, a sure-fire sale, keep them off the lists. They should be made available at once in quantity, at either public or philanthropic expense, and for both public and private schools. Knowing nature is the joy of the child as it is his right, and catastrophic current events indicate that if the child is stunted in this matter society is going to pay for the neglect.

In respect to history, art and science, we are saying two things. First, that the child can know, and secondly, that in order to live as a mature person in a modern community of persons, he needs to know. As it happens, he is being invited and forced to learn how to live in a world community. If he is left illiterate in fundamentals, he is being shortchanged and is having the wool pulled over his eyes.

The same is true when the child is left illiterate in the matter of knowing and loving God. Then he is cheated and only half introduced to man's world. Somebody has robbed him: the school or home or state or church or the bad tradition of society at large. Poor kid, he is as helpless as men locked into a concentration camp, and must charge at things as guilelessly as a Don Quixote. In the matter of knowing and loving God, at least as decisively as in knowing nature and history, the child wants to know; he can know and needs to know.

Recall the verse by Theodore Dreiser who, at the height of our progressivist as well as naturalistic era, said (in 1930) that he prayed for light on cosmic meaning: "I pray, by God, on my knees, for light—and no light is given." Dreiser, compassionate and (as he said) bewildered, was a great and gifted man, and yet a confused and tragic figure; things surely were at cross-purposes in him. Dreiser or the times had left Dreiser at half-mast. Now, the child can see more clearly than such a man, since the child can catch some glimpses of meaning and is able to know that all is somehow or other intelligible, that all makes "sense" and not nonsense. The child can absorb the first lessons in knowing that God is, and can know something, even if ever so vaguely, of what God is, as the primitive, who in some ways is more a child than we are, has always known, at least in a vague and not wholly unsatisfactory manner, that God is and something of what God is. The primitive is not religiously illiterate. He can read God in things. Even if he only knows it vaguely and inarticulately, he knows (to use John Locke's simple argument) that something absolutely is, that some greatest being exists. And knowing some absolute and greatest being, he accepts that being in an appropriate social way, by means of various ritualized gestures together with remarkably strong emotions. In his knowledge and freedom the primitive proclaims that greatest being and in his own way recognizes his essential relation to it. This acknowledgement by man of his relation to God, made, as matters of freedom always are made, in any of a dozen ways, is religion.

For a generation or so, in a growing number of influential persons, mostly in higher education and in products of it, naturalistic secularism was set against teaching religion in schools. The Protestant Bishop James A. Pike has said that religion was "downgraded" in schools and notably in colleges and universities, even by professors and presidents who personally were believers and worshippers. To profess a faith was thought to be unscientific or too bold. Or perhaps to hide one's beliefs was thought in the circumstances to be safer. The idea grew that university life must be neutral if not wholly secular, just as it was thought that legal and political and economic life had best be neutral or wholly secular. Justice Holmes was an interesting example of this secularized thinking; he often said that he took man to be a cosmic ganglion and he wanted to delete from the language all reference to the transcendent God and to sin. It was constantly assumed by highly placed educators that private as well as public high schools had better keep mum on the religious issue: Dr. Conant is an instance of this "goodbye to all that" assumption. Even in Catholic and Protestant universities it was commonly assumed that all non-theological knowledge is in essence secular.

Secularism is of course in a poor position to receive and acknowledge any kind or degree of knowledge referring to Divine Being. In passing, we repeat that in terms of total human history, man is found to be the worshipping animal. In that case, secularism can only occupy an aristocratic position. If possible at all, atheism, even more negative that agnostic secularism, is for an elite and not for mankind.

Able and ready to know God in some rudimentary way, the child has the right to know these simple things—first, about the snobbish aristocrat who says that man does not know God and thinks he himself does not worship, and second, about man, the universal democrat who has always been knowing and worshipping God. The child should know that, unless he worships, he cannot live fully as a person and cannot join in membership with the total community of humanity, as he has a right to do and we would say a duty to do. Some years ago, a lively pamphlet by Stringfellow Barr was entitled, "Let's Join the Human Race." That was and is a good idea, and that in effect is what the parent-educator, speaking with nature, says to the child when he first assists him along the road to a life of God-Worship: "Let's join the human race."

The child has a right to know these basic and simple democratic matters, just as he has a right to know history and science and to know man's essential goodness and man's evident weakness and just as he has the right to live as a person and as a member of the community of mankind.

Every man is paying the highest tribute to something, and thus, whatever his preferences and feelings, he is worshipping. The child can and should know this.

Sir Walter Moberly says * that on "the fundamental religious issue" "the modern university intends to be, and supposes it is, neutral, but it is not. Certainly, it neither inculcates nor expressly repudiates belief in God. But it does what is far more deadly than open rejection; it ignores Him." Our own view is the same. We say it is wrong and a shame to teach the child, by words or by silence, the commandment: "Thou shalt not through this school know anything about God. Thou shalt not in or through this school in any way worship God." The child is born to know and worship God and is hamstrung as a person and as a member of the community and the human race if he is kept religiously illiterate. John Gunther has reported in *Death Be Not Proud* that his son, facing death due to a brain tumor, was tongue-tied when it was a question of praying to God. Was this perhaps because the brilliant child had been kept in an abnormal environment?

Man is found everywhere and always to be the worshipping animal. Such is the report from anthropology, history and psychology. Worship is one of the pan-human universals. Always and everywhere man has been a worshipper and if one god is taken from him he will soon find another god and another worship and theology. Nature will not tolerate the vacuum. In relation to colleges, Gustave Weigel has put the matter in few words †: "The only choice given to the college is *how* it will teach theology or religion, because it will be taught no matter how negative the policy of the school. Certainly the present form of

* Sir Walter Moberly, *The Crisis in the University*, p. 55.
† Weigel, "The College and the Dimensions of Reality," *Liberal Education*, 45 (March, 1959), p. 49.

teaching it, which consists of having it bootlegged into every conceivable department, is hardly satisfactory."

In his penetrating study of Russian Communism, Berdyaev put the same point universally for peoples. He said that man can turn anything into an idol and find a way to pay divine honors to it. A stone or a tree will do, or the sun, a bull, some man, the state, science, progress, the proletariat, or humanity. We know that any of them will serve as god, because they have done so; man has worshipped each of these. No matter then what our particular convictions and likes and dislikes, man turns up, after all, a worshipper. The child in the grades and surely in high school could learn these easy factual lessons, and could see how naive was the American anthropologist (Dr. White of Michigan University) who is reported as having said that the Russians, though godless, have notably advanced in science. A child can see that all peoples have gods, and could see the naivety of Dr. White's assumption.

Of course, such lessons, at most preliminary, would be "about" religion. They would not be in any sense the practice of religion, much less would they amount to "commitment," and they would be no more sectarian indoctrination than arithmetic or geography is. Yet surely the lessons would be relevant, and all of us who are tutors and pedagogues of the human spirit may feel obliged both to learn them and to begin to teach them.

"The irreligious man is precisely the man who lives on the surface of things and recognizes no ultimate spiritual allegiance." From Christopher Dawson, whom we have just quoted, and from Toynbee and others, the child has the right to learn the lesson expressed in their many beautiful volumes. Today this lesson in history might well be one of the harder lessons, because many of us in American colleges and universities, and perhaps even in high schools, have for some time tended to accept and teach two dubious propositions. First, we have taught at least by assumption and silence that there are irreligious peoples, peoples without gods and worship. And secondly, we have taught by assumption that though religion may be all right for those who want it and enjoy it and get a sort of emotional catharsis out of it, society and civilization and the national and international life are not one iota better if men have religion or one iota worse if they have no religion. In *Religion and Culture,* Dawson, who is professor of Catholic studies at Harvard, has shown how outmoded and unrealistic those nineteenth century notions were.

As the child becomes a little more grown up, he could begin to learn these lessons, and the following closely related truths might perhaps be considered. First, the positive correlation which, as Dawson and Toynbee show, exists between religion and the national and total human good. A strong civilization presupposes a strong religion. Dawson says that a culture losing its religion is a dying culture, "no matter how prosperous" it may outwardly appear. Secondly, the difficulty, to put it mildly, in the view that it is all the same to the national good whether men have any religion. Thirdly, that, like it or lump it, the peoples of mankind have gods and do worship. And lastly, that, if the true God can be known, the knowledge and corresponding worship would be quite in the swim of democracy, in the literal sense of this word, and would be as beneficent as air.

The matter may be turned around in another way. We the citizens of any nation have the duty and therefore the right to try to build and maintain a great civilization and a great culture, and history seems to say that this cannot be done when a civilization is losing its religion. At least at the high school level, the child has the right to this bit of vital information in history and sociology.

But why all this powwow? After all, who could or would deprive the child of freedom to know and love God and thus deprive him of this vision and enlargement? We do not admit that all men could be thus robbed, or that in the long run people generally could be robbed of God and worship. Things do not work that way, in Russia or elsewhere. "Man" is sure to reassert himself; the democracy of religion will have its way. But granting that, in the light of totalities and eternities, only a relatively few could be made to suffer the loss of conscious God-contact, and for a time only, what could cause this deprivation of light and freedom? Among things depriving youths of freedom to know and worship God are the following.

First, the all-powerful state or ruler at times says, "Thou shalt not have strange gods; me only shalt thou serve." Mussolini laid down the formula for all dictators: "Everything in the state, nothing outside the state." Some Nero, Mussolini, Hitler, Stalin or Khrushchev appears at one time or another, and says this, in a slick way or a blunderbus way. Some conceivable public opinion or popular vote could say it for some time to a minority, since the tyranny of the majority is a possibility, as has been noticed by great students and lovers of freedom such as de Tocqueville, John Stewart Mill and Lord Acton. The tyranny of the majority is something that minds blinded by a chauvinist god could scarcely see.

The first hindrance therefore to freedom of knowing and worshipping God is the omnipotent state in one form or another. The primacy goes to the god Caesar.

Secondly, secularist teaching, which, like any teaching, easily turns into dogma, could become bumptious and begin to say: "Thou shalt not know and worship." This seems to mean just what it says. What it really means is that man is asked to transfer allegiance and worship to the gods specified by secularism—the state perhaps, or some man, or reason and progress and science, or the improvement of society. Communism is revolutionary secularism, and it has its gods to which all must bow, such gods as the divine Lenin or Stalin or the old-fashioned Marxist's coming might of the proletariat. Secularism may vary the theme and carry the fight to more indigenous grounds, invoking the immunity of the flag. It may claim that our national political life is secularistic by constitutional fiat and public schools therefore must be kept secularized. Or it may rest on quieter and more circumspectly sceptical grounds, historically most plausibly adduced in the Western world, we remark in passing, by the sensism of David Hume.

Thirdly, secularism may rest on a vague scientism as we claim it did in Dewey's thought, and as it obviously does in Julian Huxley's. The Huxley position is that we know only through science, and presumably science does not reach God. Positivism is secularistic. In America the name given to secularism is "naturalism," an inept word since all philosophy is natural and since the philosophy of the necessarily "natural" Plato and Aristotle was not secularistic "naturalism." George F. Thomas has said * that, according to secularism-naturalism, "reality is identical with nature as the totality of things and events in space and time. There is no eternal, super-sensible, spiritual world that transcends the natural order." Secularism accepts beliefs and worship as facts, only to try to rationalize them and thus get rid of them, or again only to claim that they are "meaningless" phenomena, their bases not empirically verifiable.

* George F. Thomas, "Religious Perspectives in College Teaching." Hazen Foundation, New Haven, Conn., 1951.

Fourthly, some American pragmatists used to keep repeating that religion is impractical, that it distracts energy from social service, that ultimates are irrelevant, that perhaps God could be proved in one way or another if we were not so rushed with a lot of things to do. That in sum was Dewey's reiterated doctrine for years, and he finally summarized his position. In 1933, Dewey said in the *Christian Century* that we are too busy to go proving God as cause or as orderer, and a year later in his Yale lectures, *A Common Faith,* he drew the logical conclusion. The identification of our values, he said, "with the creeds and cults of religion must be dissolved"—a demand for liquidation: *Carthago delenda est.* That vigorous conclusion made clear two points in Dewey's philosophy: that it was a monistic and naturalistic absolutism, and that Dewey's general as well as his educational theory was unfriendly to religious literacy.

Fifthly, a whole kit of distractions, nuisances and scandals can get the notion of God and the practice of worship out of men's lives; e.g., a blind, reactionary position on the part of religionists: either a dour Calvinist doctrine, such as that in Reinhold Niebuhr's thought, or a fundamentalist doctrine of the William Jennings Bryan variety, or an extreme conservative position as held by some Catholic religious leaders on social problems. These doctrines and positions are unfair to religion. Both in its nature and as it works out in history, religion is at once a revolutionary force creating civilizations and a conservative force sustaining them. But sometimes some of its leaders in various nations, including our own, have the look of being against every good thing.

In short, youths in schools can be kept from learning about God and from worshipping by scandal and false preachers, by custom and the mores, by ignorance and inhibitions, or by some power group: the Politburo, the democratic majority, the state, the professors. Our position was summarized succinctly and with power by Cuninggim who said in 1947*:

> The spirit of secularism has continued to be characteristic of the collegiate scene. All that was said before concerning secularism has persisted: that it looked upon religion as peripheral, or worse, as useless, and not intellectually respectable; that it took its cue from the general secular spirit infecting society, the materialism in practical affairs, the naturalism in science and philosophy, the humanism in religion. College professors by the hundreds, particularly in the natural sciences, thought of religion as an opiate, or at least as a sign of weakness. Dedicating themselves to the scientific method, they ignored the possibility that truth could be arrived at in any other way. Science became, in fact, a sort of religion.

On the positive side, our claim comes to this: that the child can get some rudimentary knowledge-acquaintance with God and can learn easy lessons about the necessary place of religion in the growth of nations that remain strong and healthy. These things he can and should learn at home, at church and at school. The least we may say is that the school, high or low and no matter how public or private, has no right by word or deed or silence to undermine even one child's faith in God. As the late G. K. Chalmers, who was president of Kenyon College, said in *The Republic and the Person*, the child coming into college —and experience shows that the American student leaving high school is intellectually a child—must begin cautiously

---

* Merrimon Cuninggim, *The College Seeks Religion* (Yale Studies in Religious Education). Yale University Press, 1947; pp. 23-24.

to put belief and doubt together as two vital things. In the medieval formula, the ideal of the advanced student was *credere et bene dubitare* (Chalmers took it from a later century). But, continued Chalmers, to throw the child out of a believing and worshipping home into a course in advanced scepticism is unjust to the child, the home and the republic.

We are holding for more than Chalmers' excellent statement. We hold that in all schools, the child's faith should have the chance to be nourished and developed. The child has the right to know about God and to know God. The school must do better than not stand in his way. Parents and educators in America have the right and the duty to go to work to desecularize all schools, just as people in Russia have the right, though no opportunity, to desecularize schools and society. But, in fact, is the opportunity also denied to us?

Admittedly, it is one thing to have or to declare for a right, and quite another thing to find ways for people to enjoy and exercise the right. We must come step by step to that part of our question. After we have dealt with the "separation" principle and with what can be done, people may then make up their minds whether the right to religious literacy through the schools, though surely a right, must be kept in cold storage.

CHAPTER 3

The Wall of Separation

Though in the most human senses of the words, men must keep trying to make "one world," history suggests that they will have only a relative success and that trouble and conflict will remain. One area of conflict is the church-state area, and only he who goes for a socio-temporal absolutism thinks he can get rid of it once for all. At least in the Occidental Jewish-Christian world, the confidence of souls who think they can erase the problem must seem naive. Perpetually in history the spiritual and the temporal collide, and they will continue to collide. Why must this be? The answer is simple. They jam into each other because the church has its being, its rights, its authority, its means and ends and its obligations, and so has the state. The subjects of the two co-exist in one time and one place, and all the subjects of the church are subjects of the state, and some or all subjects of the state are subjects of the church. Matters of jurisdiction are sure to come up. If fish in the sea were subject to two different laws and two different tempos, and were headed for an end transcending

57

in time and importance the temporal end of fish life, they would need bright minds and a fund of good will to keep things in order. Things as simple as jets now and then collide in the open sky.

Who then, at least among teachers, is so innocent as to think that in the topsy-turvy socio-temporal ocean the whole stream of church and state may be expected to flow all the time as smoothly as oil?

The only way to "solve" the problem would be an unsatisfactory either-or. It would be for the church to swallow the state in the manner of ancient Jewish theocracy, or for the state to try to swallow the church in the manner, for example, of Russian dictatorship.

Church and state are like dynamic bisecting geometrical figures, and for that reason the two are bound to have an occasional run-in. Once in a while the old problem turns up in the educational field, in Belgium or France or England or Nazi Germany or the United States. This is natural and inevitable, since the church has need of a say and the right and duty to have a say in the education of its citizens, all Hitlers and Stalins to the contrary notwithstanding; and the state also has need of a say and the right and duty to have a say in the education of its citizens. We repeat that the citizens of one are the citizens of the other. To pretend that the church may not have a word to say as to how its citizens are to be educated, would be like saying that the church may be and advisedly is indifferent to doctrine, to teaching, to how its members' minds are formed. The same holds for the state and the education of its citizen-members. To say that church or state may skip the problem would amount to saying that it is all the same what anybody thinks about anything, that ideas have no consequences, and that there is no correlation between thought and action.

No church with the slightest respect for itself and no state with the slightest respect for itself could suppose such a thing. An occasional flareup therefore of the church-state problem on educational or other matters is fully to be expected. It has happened, it does happen, it will happen. This circumstance is all the more likely where the church in question is either Jewish or Christian, claiming not only to express a human relation to a God transcending the state, but claiming to be a church in some way established and maintained by God. As if the situation were not difficult enough, it has been made far more complicated in our country by the presence of numerous Protestant religions lacking full accord with each other. As if the ancient, ever-new Jewish problem was not enough, or the Jewish-Christian problem or the Catholic-Protestant problem!

On the church-state-school problem, the wrangle in our country has been considerable and long-standing, and we will have more of it. The first serious shake-up was a real crisis. This developed among Protestants who were only in agreement, and this by assumption, that the public schools of America should be Protestant, but who soon fell into conflict as to which Protestant sect should dominate and have the say in schools. A careful study * reports: "The immediate cause of the exclusion of religious teaching from the schools was sectarian conflict." The conflict was not a Jewish or Catholic phenomenon, but Protestant-sectarian. The greatest protagonist of public schools, unless Jefferson himself, was Horace Mann who frankly wanted religion in public schools, without, said Mann, invading "those rights of conscience which are established by the laws of God and guaranteed to us by the Constitution of

* *The Relation of Religion to Public Education.* Washington, D.C., 1947; p. 6.

the State." * But Mann did not see a way to keep Protestant sects at peace on teaching religion in public schools, and he himself was at times violent and almost rabid on the question. Mann's greatest sufferings resulted from this problem. In his diary (June 20, 1838), he wrote: "Sunday. Both Reports in [School and Hospital]. Some efforts making by disappointed orthodoxy to disaffect the public with the Board. They want, at least some of them, their doctrines introduced. This cannot be, either theirs or those of any others, considered as sects merely." †

The late Canon Bell pointed out some years ago in *Life* (Oct. 16, 1950), that the crisis among Protestant sects precipitated the rapid spread of the neutral or what is often called the "secular" public-school system in America. It led to a situation which few desire and from which we would like by this time to extricate ourselves—the situation where most of our schools find themselves totally unable or unfree to teach religion or so much as to teach about religion.

One has only to mention such a school as Newton High in Boston or New Trier in Chicago or to consult Dr. Conant's somewhat whitewashed report on the high school, to see that some public schools are very good. If we have to admit that, all in all, our schools, public and private, on all levels, really are weak, then they must be built up. They must be built up in their own quality and in the minds of the people, since it is clear to all but the most

* Words of Horace Mann. See Raymond B. Culver, *Horace Mann and Religion in the Massachusetts Public Schools.* Yale University Press, 1929; p. 207.

† See William Kailer Dunn, *What Happened to Religious Education?* Baltimore: Johns Hopkins Press, 1958; pp. 138-143. Dunn says (p. 189) that eventually the problem became to find "a way to keep religion in and keep sectarianism out." The problem no doubt remains.

prejudiced that public and private schools are necessary to the freedom and the general good of the nation. However, no matter what the over-all quality of American schools, the trouble is that up to now the public schools have been unable to meet an inevitable problem, the problem of teaching religion in schools. We may no longer simply try to duck out of the problem.

From grade one through grade twelve, what is a child to learn about God or even about what Protestants and Catholics and Jews believe about God? At least until lately, most of us have for generations been mum on that difficult question.

The question has been a hot one for a long time. Anyone glancing at the record in magazines in the 1880's, say in the defunct *Forum* and the *Atlantic Monthly,* will see that the reactions at that time as well as in Mann's time were lively on the church-state-school question and on religion in public schools. Today the troubles have not notably let up. For the past generation, troubles of a church-state-school kind have been such a challenge that several of them reached the federal Supreme Court, and it is a safe bet that, given our situation and background, more of them are going to reach it. The air is far from cleared.

Our own hope, not an unfounded one, is that we may be on the edge of a new development of the old problem. More teachers are seeing that some teaching on religion as well as on arithmetic and geography is a necessity for the good of the social body and also as an objective presentation of given social realities. It is pretty hard to keep coming up to major social realities, and then finding a way to dodge them. The realities with their load of problems will come back on us. "Nothing elemental in human life can be indefinitely isolated in this fashion," said Dr. Johnson and his Committee. It is unrealistic and unscientific to try to seal off from the child big social institutions such as the family, the church, the state, and still say that we are scientific pedagogues. A small percentage, but, as we get farther out into villages and into rural areas, a larger percentage of parents is asking for "some religion in the schools." Often they manage to get it, too. Naturally, in public schools all that may in reason and justice be expected is some teaching about religion, not the practice of and commitment to religion, much less to a particular religion.

The legislative and legal cases going all the way to the highest court are of great interest. Let us review some of them. Following the smoke of war and under guise of patriotism, Nebraska passed a law in 1919 to the effect that no teacher might teach any subject to anyone, in Nebraska's "private, denominational parochial" schools, in any language except English. The law really was going to be rough on anyone wanting to teach languages or to learn them!

That unhappy result would be a suffered and not a desired effect. What was wanted was something else. It was discovered that it was not educational or patriotic good that prompted the law, but an animus toward local Catholic and Lutheran parochial schools, several of which did in fact teach some subjects in German. In 1922, the voters of Oregon did much the same and for the same reason. They decided by a vote of 115,506 to 103,685 that Oregon children, ages eight to sixteen—unless special circumstances such as cost to the state happened to intervene—should after September, 1926, be required by heavy fines, levied on parents or guardians, to attend public schools.

In each case, patriotism and the flag were in the forefront of the stated reason for the enactment, and even the

most unfriendly visitor tramping through those common-
wealths at that time must have caught himself envying
the devotion to flag and country. He would be made to
feel that Nebraska and Oregon were the native homes of
freedom.

In each case the Supreme Court of the United States
unanimously declared the law unconstitutional, a violation
of citizen rights guaranteed under the Fourteenth Amendment.

Before citing more recent cases which also are of great
interest, let us look at what is, at least to all appearances,
an unbiased review of the Nebraska one-language law and
the Oregon public-schools-only law.

Writing in *The Survey* for July 1, 1925, Robert W. Bruère
sized up the general social problems involved as follows.
The argument from patriotism, he said, had been the
argument back of the Oregon law just then disqualified.
It was argued that children should be kept under the
exclusive tutelage of the state from eight to sixteen, since
only thus could undivided allegiance to flag and country
be established in their minds. "The avowed purpose of
the law, as developed by the State and the courts," said
Bruère, "was to buttress patriotism in the young and to
insure their single-minded allegiance to the Flag and the
Constitution . . . The Oregon law was one of a recent
series through which attempts have been made to do by
indirection what could not constitutionally be accomplished
directly. It was inspired not so much by high scientific and
educational considerations as by a determination to use
the schools as artillery in a religious controversy which
dates back to the Middle Ages and which persists as a
political issue in spite of the Constitution and the courts . . .
The non-denominational private schools were caught in the
net of political expediency; the main object of the legislation

as avowed during the campaign in its behalf, was to curb the Roman Catholic schools whose influence, it was alleged, tended to divide the children's allegiance between the sovereignty of the Church and the sovereignty of the State."

This Oregon case, then, if Bruère's view was correct, was a flare-up of an old and dangerous fire, one of the liveliest flare-ups that we have suffered in the twentieth century. This was the old fire and ruse of turning political power into a means of promoting denominational religious ends, and this is a subtle form of self-deception which is the eternal temptation of any dominant religious group. We must note in passing that just this sort of thing keeps recurring in Oregon and elsewhere and that the POAU, perhaps quite unconsciously, is in effect dogmatically committed to it; and let us mention, also in passing, that the POAU was politically busy as recently as 1958 in the same kind of save-the-nation and save-the-Constitution campaign. In 1958 the zealot's fight was to abrogate an Oregon law allowing tax money for textbooks for children in private and parochial schools. Of the 1958 Oregon campaign by POAU and others, Governor Holmes of Oregon said: "To deprive those schools of free books would be discriminating against youngsters in those schools. I think those protesting the law are taking a bigoted view"; and a state senator, himself a Methodist, said: "The real purpose of most of those against the law is to abolish the private and parochial school systems." In line with the Oregon efforts have been the repeated efforts of POAU and others in California to require private and parochial grade and high schools to pay taxes, a requirement which would run contrary to all American tradition.

So much for the troubles of 1958. We return to those of 1925. In the Catholic schools of Oregon, religious instruction had been given and moral training afforded according to the tenets of the Catholic Church. The decision of our highest court, delivered in 1925 by Justice McReynolds, found such instruction and training to be so far from inimical to the rights of parents or the good of the state that they were said to be "a kind of undertaking not inherently harmful, but long regarded as useful and meritorious."

As for the effect of the decision, it is quite clear, now, that Robert Bruère was too optimistic in that 1925 *Survey* article, and perhaps he was guilty of wishful thinking. This is what he said: "The effect of the decision is to check the use of the public schools as a partisan weapon in a political controversy waged about an issue lying outside their recognized orbit." Issues on politics, on religion and on the schools were all mixed up, according as the confusion appeared to be of immediate advantage to the groups mixing them, and the expediency principle counted for more than the good of the child or the nation. Patriotism was used as an expedient weapon by church people who waved the flag as if they meant it. They seemed to be divinely commissioned to protect the flag. The good of political unity was another chief appeal used by these people: unless a nation had one school system it would suffer divisiveness and be torn to pieces. Such undercover tactics, said Bruère, would be checked by the Supreme Court decisions.

Bruère saw the Nebraska one-language law of 1919 in the same light. "In this case," he said, "the Supreme Court not only defended educational freedom, but also restrained the political majority from using the public schools as a weapon in a controversy in which legitimate educational considerations were involved only indirectly and as a matter of larger political strategy . . . Here again the law had a specific animus although its language was general and inclusive." The animus, he said, was this: the law was apparently directed against the teaching and use of German, and in this regard, it would be a hang-over from World War I hysteria, but the law was in fact intended to put a stop to the teaching and use of German in Catholic and Lutheran parochial schools.* The case was carried to the Supreme Court in the name of a teacher named Meyer who had been found guilty in the state court of having taught religion in German to children during the noon recess. The Nebraska law also was unanimously declared unconstitutional.

Even if we grant a levelling and persecuting instinct as a kind of sadism in persons and groups, the animus back of the Nebraska and Oregon controversies is instructive relative to the controversies of later decades. An anti-Catholic-Protestant feeling, a throw-back to some earlier era and (one might think) with no place in our time or at all in America, appears to have animated the drive for the Nebraska law and the Oregon law. That was the type of issue, not a scientific or an educational one, nor a patriotic issue, but a throw-back, an atavistic type of issue.

Nevertheless for some years now the ground has shifted. More markedly than a generation ago, the drive has recently been secularism against all religion, though still vigorously carried on is the drive against private and parochial schools. The odd thing, in a way, is that some Protestants, perhaps not deeply religious or American ones, have gone with the secularist animus and drive. Naturally, many Protestant persons and groups have declared them-

* The law forbade "teachers in any private, denominational parochial school [to] teach any subject to any person in any language other than the English language" and prohibited the teaching of any foreign language to any pupil until he had completed the eighth grade.

selves ashamed of the vigorous, anti-Catholic, and what we can only think un-American, feeling and actions of Protestants and Other Americans United for Separation of Church and State. In the present matter, this group of zealots falls in with secularism and with the revolutionary secularism which is Communism.

In much of the more recent propaganda, patriotism and undivided allegiance have continued to be used as the whip. The implication is that the number one god must be Caesar. Notice how much the ends and the methods, as stated both before the courts and in popular declarations, run along consistent lines:

First— All parochial schools should be checked.—The Nebraska law, 1919.

Second—All private and parochial grade schools should be debarred.—The Oregon law, 1922.

Third— All private high schools, "religious" or "economic," should be "smoked out."—James B. Conant, 1952.

Fourth—All private and parochial grade and high schools should be taxed.—Californians for Public Schools, 1958.

The overt argument is the same: the Flag, the Constitution, unity, undivided allegiance. The means is the same: the supression of freedom to operate private schools at some or all levels, suppression directly by legislation and court fiat or indirectly through authorities and public opinion. The end is not the same. The secularist wants secularism—that is all he can want. The nativist wants nativism as itself a kind of religion.

The nativist says he wants to save American freedom and the goods of democracy from powerful foreign enemies. But it might seem to the innocent outsider as if the nativist wants freedom in some sort of special way and for special people.* In practice he tends to dilute and destroy what he says he wants to preserve. He says the other fellow is seeking to get political power and to abrogate freedom. So he takes no chances. If possible, he seizes power and abrogates freedom, and says the other fellow is dangerous and anti-democratic.

In this matter, many Jews have been standing with secularism, since, reversing their common position of two decades ago, they are vociferous against religion in public schools as un-American and unconstitutional. The Jews' case nevertheless seems to us more intelligible. Many Jews teach religion very well outside school, and if religion comes in one form or another into the public schools we can surmise that Protestants stand to gain most and Jews to gain least. Besides, Jews always suffer discrimination, notably in regard to schools and to employment, and have reason to be afraid of new occasions for it. All the same, it may be regarded as a dissembling when Jews claim to be so eagle-eyed that they are able to find in the Constitution something that others do not readily find there, and when they purport to be the greatest Constitution-defending patriots. They simply have an axe to grind. They want to protect Jewish thought and life from exposure, in public schools, to Christian presuppositions.

What, then, about the "separation principle"? What about the "wall" which we have been so careful to erect and maintain for more than a century and a half, ever since the First Amendment—article one of the Bill of Rights— was adopted by the First Congress, or at least since President Thomas Jefferson used the "wall of separation" metaphor in a letter? Did not Jefferson then make history, and

* That in fact is what a till-then insider said of the POAU when he broke from the group in 1958.

who wants to wipe out history? It is un-American to go against "the wall." But does not he who wants private schools, above all private schools on a religious basis, and who perhaps asks help for "supplementary" and welfare services, for the finest teacher training, for polio shots for children in those schools, and for books and bus rides and hot lunches for them, does not he want to break down "the wall"? Does he not prove himself a foreigner and transgressor? Does not he want to break down "the wall" who wants religion taught in any form in the public schools on any level, or to have children released from school to study religion? Is not he an unpatriotic wall-smasher who wants to promote studies in religion and theology at great universities such as Harvard and Michigan University? After all, is not the latter a state university, heavily tax-supported?

We might well pity the courts, for they too, as we shall now see, have found this multiple question sufficiently embarrassing. The Nebraska and the Oregon law were fought and decided on grounds of freedom and property rights, under the Fourteenth and not the First Amendment. In delivering the court's opinion in the Oregon case, Justice McReynolds went farther than (we might think) necessary. He said that to deny to parents the right to choose schools, private or public, for their children would be to proceed on a theory of the state foreign to ours. The right to make the choice, he said, belongs to the parents and not to the state, always presupposing that minimum state requirements are met. Justice McReynolds went so far as to say in that public document that, no matter what any law or constitution says, parents have a natural right in regard to the education of their children; "the right," he said, "coupled with the high responsibility."

Later decisions of the federal Supreme Court from 1929

through 1952 have been based on a different ground. The Louisiana textbook case, the New Jersey school bus case, the McCollum released time case, and the Zorach released time case have been decided on the basis of the First Amendment, which is the first article of the Bill of Rights. This article reads: "Congress shall make no law respecting an establishment of religion, or prohibiting the free exercise thereof."

The Louisiana law allowed the state to furnish textbooks in nonreligious subjects to children in private religious schools. The federal Supreme Court decided in 1929 that the law was constitutional. But in so deciding, it did more than sanction that particular law. It declared, for the first time, the child's rights and the state's rights in these matters. It said that not the school, and by inference not the church, but the child and the state are the beneficiaries when textbooks are furnished out of tax money. These are the words of the Supreme Court: "The schools, however, are not the beneficiaries of these appropriations. They obtain nothing from them, nor are they relieved of a single obligation because of them. *The school children and the state alone are the beneficiaries.*" (Italics ours.)

The principle thus declared by the federal Supreme Court is of vast importance for the good of the child and the nation.* It was and it will be of importance also in

---

* Before the 1958 politico-religious rumpus in California, the California Supreme Court had, on the same "public purpose" grounds, upheld a state law exempting private schools from taxes. The Court said: "Under any circumstances, any benefit received by religious denominations is merely incidental to the achievement of a public purpose." The decision on the Connecticut school-bus law on June 13, 1960, by the state Supreme Court, allowed communities to let buses carry children to nonprofit private schools. In delivering the opinion of the Court, Chief Justice Baldwin said that the statute "aids parents in sending their children to a school of their choice, as is their right. It protects the children from the dangers of modern traffic. . . ."

regard to later decisions, for instance on bus rides to private schools.

The New Jersey law was much like the Louisiana law, since it allowed school children going to private parochial schools to ride buses paid for by tax money. But the decision of the Supreme Court in its favor has caused more discussion; in fact, for many years we will keep picking up reverberations from the decision. In numerous places in several states the "public" school bus—so called to distinguish it from a school bus—has been passing up children going to private religious schools, much as if the "public" fire truck should pass up the burning Baptist church or the burning house of a Presbyterian, or as if some groups of citizens were to be denied, for religious reasons, the use of the "public" highway when they set out for church: the argument would be that church and state get tangled up when sectarians use the highway or the fire truck or school bus, though of course it is true that citizens and the state are in each instance the beneficiaries.

The decision of the federal Supreme Court in the Everson or New Jersey bus case (1947) was that the state might use "public" tax money to furnish children a way to go to private denominational schools.*

An interesting and obvious turn of the case for the children's use of the "public" school bus was the argument from non-discrimination: if bus service out of tax money for some children, why not for all children? Put rhetorically the argument would run: Whose money, whose bus, whose road is this? Generalized, the decision recognizes that discrimination in the application of public welfare benefits

---

* A variation of the "anti" feeling appeared in Sioux City, Iowa when, in the summer of 1952, polio was rampant in that area. People thought that carting kids daily to a lake might protect them; but patriotic citizens put Catholic-school children off the bus marked "public" school bus.

is unconstitutional. For that reason, the 1960 school-aid bill, if passed by Congress and the President, might not stand a Supreme Court test.

The McCollum case is the most famous of all. The Champaign, Illinois, practice was judged (1948) by the Supreme Court of the United States to be unconstitutional. The practice at Champaign had been for Jewish, Catholic and Protestant religious teachers * to teach denominational religion one hour a week in the public-school buildings. It was decided that this practice was contrary to the First Amendment which says that "Congress shall make no law respecting an establishment of religion, or prohibiting the free exercise thereof."

Evidently, Congress had in this instance done just that —passed a law either respecting an establishment of religion or prohibiting the free exercise thereof, though many people, including Justice Reed of the Supreme Court and some constitutional lawyers such as Edwin S. Corwin of Princeton and Arthur E. Sutherland, Jr., then of Cornell, later of Harvard Law School, wondered at the decision and thought it farfetched. In dissenting, Justice Reed said these things: 1. I cannot find what it is in the McCollum case that is unconstitutional. 2. What is prohibited by the decision is religious instruction of public-school children, in the school, during school hours. 3. The history of American education is against such an interpretation. 4. Is the practice of giving the aforesaid instruction a law "respecting an establishment of religion"?

Justice Black delivered the majority opinion in the McCollum case, and Justice Reed and the experts just mentioned found the decision and both the language and the theory of it difficult. Justice Black said: The facts "show

* By the time the suit was brought, classes by Jews in Jewish religion had ceased.

the use of tax-supported property for religious instruction and the close cooperation between the school authorities and the religious council in promoting religious education. The operation of the State's compulsory education system thus assists and is integrated with the program of religious instruction carried on by separate religious sects. Pupils compelled by law to go to school for secular instruction are released in part from their legal duty upon condition that they attend the religious classes. This is beyond all doubt a utilization of the tax-supported and tax-established public school system to aid religious groups to spread their faith. And it falls squarely under the ban of the First Amendment (made applicable to the States by the Fourteenth) as we interpreted it in *Everson v. Board of Education*." * Neither state nor federal government, Justice Black concluded in 1948 as in 1947, "can pass laws which aid one religion, aid all religions, or prefer one religion over another."

This final triadic statement was surprising, since it has always been the custom of both the states and the nation to collaborate with religion and in that way to aid religion, now this religion, now that one, and sometimes all religions. It is true, of course, that we have not had and may not have an established national church, and at least in that sense we have "separation" of church and state. But under the Constitution we have had established state churches, and continued, advisedly or not, to have one in Massachusetts until 1833. Having a national church is one thing, and favoring a particular church is a closely related thing. Aiding and promoting religion, as a part of aiding citizens and the common good, is quite another matter. Like aiding

* In the Everson case, the Court had said: "Neither a State nor the Federal Government can set up a church. Neither can pass laws which aid one religion, aid all religions, or prefer one religion over another."

and promoting business or publishing or farming or railroading, it is something that on occasion the state may
find itself obliged to do; and it has been the common
American practice for the state to aid religion, as well as
to aid business, publishing,* farming, and railroading. In
both his *Religion and Education Under the Constitution*
and his *Catholicism and American Freedom,* James M.
O'Neill, then of Brooklyn College, asserted that all our
presidents have acted on the assumption that the First
Amendment allows impartial governmental aid to religion.
"Every Congress, without a single exception," said Professor O'Neill, "has used public money in the promotion of
religious activities . . . Not only have all presidents and
all Congresses used public money in aid of religion and religious education, but every state in the Union, from the
day of its beginning, has used tax-supported facilities and
personnel, cooperating with religion and religious education." †

If this is so, Justice Black's statement that it is illegal to
"aid one religion" is out of line with American history, as
is his statement that it is illegal to "aid all religions." Only
his statement that it is illegal "to prefer one religion over
another" has sanction in American legal and constitutional
history.

At least for some judges in the Supreme Court the Mc-
Collum decision was a difficult one to render. Let us see
how they took sides. In a special concurrence, Justice Jackson said that we cannot find one word in the Constitution
or in any legal source to help us make the decision as to
where the secular ends and the sectarian begins in educa-

---

* The federal government has, time out of mind, aided news-
papers, magazines and ads by carrying and delivering them at a loss
in the U.S. mails.

† James M. O'Neill, *Catholicism and American Freedom.* New
York: Harper, 1952; pp. 48-49.

tion. There is available, he said, "no law but only our own prepossessions." He said that if the courts are going to take up and decide every variation of the controversy, they are likely to have much business in this line and that the wall of separation in the present matter is a winding wall. Granting that we should disallow formal instruction and "teaching of creed and catechism and ceremonial" and proselytising in schools, he asked whether it is possible "to isolate and cast out of secular education" all "religious education." Perhaps it is possible, he said, in mathematics and chemistry, but can we do so in literature and arts and history? His reply is classic and makes good sense as philosophy of education. Here are his words. "The fact is that, for good or for ill, nearly everything in our culture worth transmitting, everything that gives meaning to life, is saturated with religious influences, derived from paganism, Judaism, Christianity—both Catholic and Protestant—and other faiths accepted by a large part of the world's peoples. One can hardly respect a system of education that would leave the student wholly ignorant of the currents of religious thought."

Justice Reed alone wholly dissented and said with some warmth that at this rate the Court would have to get rid of all oaths, all chaplaincies, etc.; by implication he was asking whether the Court was prepared to go through with its own logic. In a special concurrence (along with Burton, Jackson and Rutledge), Justice Frankfurter said that "separation" means the requirement to "abstain from fusing functions of Government and of religious sects . . . We find that the basic Constitutional principle of absolute Separation was violated." He also said that long before the Fourteenth Amendment, "The prohibition of furtherance by the State of religious instruction became the guiding principle, in law and feeling, of the American people."

On seeing this assertion, Professor Arthur E. Sutherland, Jr., said the Justice was over-simplifying—everything the Justice said needed qualification.

In a remarkable study, Dr. Sutherland proceeded to remark, quite at variance with Justice Frankfurter, that readers in the history of church and state must be struck by two long-established American traditions. One is an intimate association between government and religion. The other is a symbiosis of church and school. Though each tradition has waned, the ancient tradition associating religion with education dies hard. Note for instance the invocation by the minister at most graduation exercises, and songs with religious motifs at Thanksgiving and Christmas, not to mention "America" and "The Star Spangled Banner." Hence, he concluded, the naiveté and romantic character of Justice Frankfurter's assertion.

Along with Justice Reed, Dr. Sutherland wondered how far we want this clipping tendency to go. He remarked that, as he wrote, a school director (possibly himself) had just been visiting a public grade school. The visitor came upon the tots in the act of violating the "separation" principle. It was just before Christmas, and the children had pasted on the walls laden camels, and wise men, and a star with spreading rays, and cut-outs of a canonized Lycian bishop of the early Christian church, named Nicholas. Any good Carrie Nation secularist would have torn those pictures from the wall, and in regard to such emblems many a secularist is a Carrie Nation. Dr. Sutherland asked: Must the U.S. send marshals to scrape the children's pasted pictures off the schoolroom walls?

The observation of Dr. Sutherland and Justice Reed is that it is not easy to know where political wisdom leaves off and silliness begins, and they suggested that perhaps the Court had already passed the point. Dr. Sutherland is one among many legal experts who would not want to have to make the decision and say exactly where the federal government shall proscribe state encouragement of religious activity. He says the decision must be difficult, because some governmental recognition and backing of religious activity has been customary and continues with surprising vigor. For example, U.S. funds are used to support religious missions and schools for Indians, to support GI students, some of whom are in a Jewish, Catholic or Protestant seminary and are studying to become clergymen; U.S. funds are used to support GI girls becoming nuns and to support denominational colleges while they do research; federal funds for research purposes are being poured into denominational colleges; almost everywhere in America the state provides tax advantages for religious organizations; New York State among others commands school buses to carry children to Catholic parochial schools; coins bear "In God we trust," reminding us of divinity; the government prints copies of the Declaration of Independence asserting as a self-evident truth that the Creator has endowed man with unalienable rights; governors and the President back "Religious Emphasis Week" and issue proclamations urging people to give thanks to God. Shall we declare all such activities unconstitutional, or shall the courts decide "by some sort of rough justice" which activities are allowable and which are to be stopped because of the First and the Fourteenth Amendment? *

The decision in the Zorach or New York case about teaching religion during released time (1952) again showed

* Arthur E. Sutherland, Jr., "Due Process and Disestablishment," *Harvard Law Review*, v. 62, June 1949, pp. 1306-1344. Dr. Sutherland supplied several of the instances just cited. Another remarkable article on the problem is Wilber G. Katz's "Freedom of Religion and State Neutrality," *Univ. of Chicago Law Review*, v. 20, Spring 1953, pp. 426ff.

that insiders like Justice Reed and sympathetic outsiders like Professor Sutherland had difficulty in deciding where to draw the line. Four years earlier the Court had ruled in the McCollum case that the use of public classrooms to teach denominational religions is unconstitutional, but in the New York case it ruled that it is not unconstitutional to let students out of public school, at their parents' unsolicited written request, to go elsewhere in order to get religious instruction. The decision was split, 6 to 3, and famous Justices gave their opinions with a good deal of heat.

The decision looked to many laymen and to some of the Justices like a reversal of the McCollum decision, at least as the latter was literally delivered by Justice Black, who had said in part that neither any state nor the federal government "can pass laws which aid one religion, aid all religions, or prefer one religion over another." (Black was one of the outright dissenters in the New York case.) In delivering the opinion of the Court in the New York case, Justice Douglas, so it seemed to many, repudiated Justice Black's absolute assertion. Here are the words of Justice Douglas:

> We are a religious people whose institutions presuppose a supreme being. When the state encourages religious instruction or cooperates with religious authorities by adjusting the schedule of public events to sectarian needs, it follows the best of our traditions.
> To hold that it may not would be to find in the Constitution a requirement that the government show a callous indifference to religious groups. That would be preferring those who believe in no religion over those who do believe.

For a generation and more, secularists had been reading

secularism into the Constitution, and in that sense Justice Frankfurter's statement about the non-furtherance of religious instruction was correct. Justice Douglas, however, was careful to say simply that secularism was not there and, again quite simply, that "we are a religious people." To find in the Constitution "a callous indifference to religion" and to crown secularism as the American religion, he said, would be to miss the best in our traditions. To many people, Justice Douglas seemed to be merely returning to the Constitution and to American history and to what is called the American way. At any rate, he said there was no reason to read into the Bill of Rights "a philosophy of hostility to religion." Now some have thought that this was exactly what Justice Black had done in the McCollum case, and also that much uncritical though influential public opinion, even among educators, had long been moving in that direction. All of a sudden, things were unmistakably reversed: if the Zorach decision was a good one, the McCollum decision was a bad one. In fact, one criticism of the McCollum decision itself right from the start, by both Catholics and Protestants, was that by legal fiat it had attempted to make secularism the official established religion of the United States, and in a careful study, reprinted several times in various journals, Professor Corwin of Princeton had said that in that decision the Court was trying to turn itself into the national school board.

In any event, if the Zorach decision fails to allow religion *in* public schools, it does seem to open the door to a sympathetic official view of the relation of religion to the education provided by the state. The Zorach decision seems not only to mesh far better with freedom and the American way and with the natural right noted by Justice McReynolds in the Oregon case, but to be an encouragement to the many who hope something can be done by a free and intelligent people toward solving the problem of "religion and the public schools."

Not all aspects of the "separation" principle, if it may be called a principle, are yet settled, and on the school question among others some new and acute headaches are in store for both the people and the courts. Is there really any "separation" principle? In spite of much popular language to the contrary, we hold that, taken in a literal sense, there is no such principle, either in historical fact or in good theory. We do not want church and state "separated" and we have never had them "separated" and do not have them "separated" today. We have disestablishment—no established church in the nation, and now for a long time none in any state. In that modified sense of "separation," we may say with the late Canon Anson Phelps Stokes' famous work on church and state in America that the so-called "separation" is a real, though a "friendly" one.

Church and state work together in many matters, they have done so, they do, and they will. We do not mean "church" in the sense of either an established or a preferred church, but "church" in the sense of religion and also in the sense of the "all religions" debarred by Justice Black. Church and state collaborate, cooperate, work together.

If that is so, in a literal sense there is no "separation" between them, and there is no "separation principle."

Why, then, do so many intelligent people, including some teachers, think there is, and why do Justices such as Jackson, Frankfurter and Black appeal to a "separation" principle? The clumsy and misleading usage grew up out of an historical accident, and possibly some "politicking" persons and groups will continue to make the most of it for ideological and party reasons. Jefferson was the first to use the "wall of separation" metaphor. Writing, January 1, 1801, to a Baptist association then meeting at Danbury, Connecticut, President Jefferson said: "Believing with you that religion is a matter which lies solely between man and his God, that he owes account to none other for his faith or his worship, that the legislative powers of government reach actions only, and not opinions, I contemplate with sovereign reverence that act of the whole American people which declared that their legislature should 'make no law respecting an establishment of religion, or prohibiting the free exercise thereof,' thus building a wall of separation between Church and State."

Jefferson's catchy phrase was unfortunate, though of course he knew what he was talking about. He and others had in this regard fought for two things and had got them into the Constitution: first, that religion should be free from political interference, and secondly, that America should be free of any established or preferred religion.

"Separation" in a literal sense is not good theory, would not be good in fact and has always been out in fact. It would be difficult, to say the least, to erect the "wall of separation" metaphor into a legal and constitutional principle. As it happens, it has been lifted out of a famous man's letter and is no part of the Constitution. It has no more constitutional force than a metaphor lifted out a letter by any president, such as Lincoln, Wilson or Grant; that is, it has no legal or constitutional force at all.

For good or for ill, this figure of speech is lodged in the popular mind. It is established in teachers' minds as if it were written into the Constitution, and for a long time it has been confusing and misleading the public as well as the teachers. The ancients thought there were fixed stars. The idea was erroneous, but for centuries it had an immensely confusing and misleading effect. At present, one of the fixed stars with us is the idea that "separation" or "wall of separation" is in the Constitution. Even men on the Supreme Bench use misleading language which seems to presuppose such a wall. In the McCollum case, Justice Jackson spoke of "the wall of separation between Church and State," and Justice Frankfurter said that there was agreement that "the First Amendment was designed to erect a 'wall of separation between Church and State'," and in the Zorach case of 1952 Justice Jackson spoke of the "wall which the court was professing to erect." This high-placed confusion does far more harm than good, and with Dr. Sutherland and others one may well be shocked at its naiveté. The very wording is unmanageable if offered as legal and constitutional language, and from case to case it goes from bad to worse.

In the Zorach case, dissenting Justices said that the majority opinion gave "not separation but combination of church and state." The word "combination" also is wrong for either the theory or the fact. What we want in theory and what we have in fact is not separation or combination nor identification, but distinction and collaboration.

We must not confuse "unity" and "collaboration" with "identity." Unified is not identified. Man and wife form a unity, but neither is identical with the other. Here, collaboration implies neither identity nor separation. Man and wife collaborate in many matters. There is collaboration, therefore not separation. Citizens of a state are neither identical with each other nor totally separated. They form a real and important unity and of course they collaborate.

Unity between an animal's body and soul is not identity. The distinction between them is real—one cannot be reduced to the other or be the other. The two are unified, and distinct, but not separate. They collaborate, and if a wall were erected between them, the animal would at once be dead.

Distinction between nation and nation is one thing. Strict separation and non-collaboration would be quite another.

We have reason to hate iron curtains, to say nothing of "walls"—between man and wife, between nation and nation, between citizen and citizen. There is no better ground for a "wall" between church and state. The only ground is that it is difficult for them to collaborate. But it is difficult at times for man and wife to collaborate, or for nation and nation or citizen and citizen. Every day proves the difficulty in each of the instances. "Difficult to do" does not prove that it is not good to do, or that we are not bound, even in face of great difficulties, to try to collaborate.

An established church, even a favored church, would be something else. This is forbidden by the Bill of Rights. It is clear that in theory we do not want any established or any favored church, and that is all that is meant when a scholar such as Dr. Katz or Canon Stokes or Father Robert Drinan says or supposes that there is a something still unfortunately to be called "separation." The condition of disestablishment is constitutional and American, and it is a long time since we have had an established church and then only on the level of particular states. Difficult as it naturally is in practice, we must also go on doing our best not to favor any particular church.

In church-state relations as in other matters, the confusing of "separation" and "distinction" has led us and can only lead us into confusing results. A man who could not stand bunk or muddlement, Morris R. Cohen, put the issue simply *: "The failure to discriminate between *distinguish-*

* Morris R. Cohen, *Reason and Law.* Glencoe, Ill.: The Free Press, 1950; p. 160.

ing and *separation* is one of the great obstacles to the advancement of real understanding."

In our view, one of the best statements ever made on American schools and "separation" is that by Professor Paul G. Kauper of Michigan University law school. His summary is so well informed and so well balanced that we are happy to conclude this chapter with it. Dr. Kauper says *:

> The majority opinion in the *Zorach* case restored what appeared to many to be a sound perspective and judgment in the interpretation of the separation principle regarded as a constitutional mandate. The matter of separation cannot be approached in terms of verbal absolutes. Nor can a metaphor such as "the wall of separation" serve as an aid to analysis. The truth is that religion and government have been and continue to be interrelated, and that by hypothesis it is impossible to describe this situation in terms of "absolute and complete separation." Religious groups often exert a powerful influence in shaping government policy, and the spiritual and moral influences generated by religious forces have an important impact upon our national character and public life. In turn government has contributed much to religion. Our history bears witness to the numerous ways in which government has employed its powers and processes to provide more favorable opportunities for the exercise of religious freedom and the pursuit of religious interests without impinging upon the freedom of the nonbeliever and without giving a preference to a

---

* Paul G. Kauper, contributing to *Religion and the State University*, edited by Erich A. Walter. Ann Arbor: University of Michigan Press, 1958; p. 76.

single religious group. The idea that the separation principle means that government cannot "aid" religion, if stated as a universal proposition, is not supported by precedent, history, or the common understanding.

CHAPTER 4

Pluralism in Education

As is well known, a devastating feature of totalitarian regimes is the educational feature. In general, such a regime
says: "Everybody line up: everybody learn what and when
and where and as the State says." In an immediate sense,
the police and the military control people and things, but
in the long run "public schools only" are really second in
command to the dictator in controlling and shaping the
destinies of men kept under the iron heel. Nothing is more
important for state control, and no genuine Hitler or Stalin
could think of tolerating any schools set up by or operated
by truly free citizens. That is understood. Mussolini was
bold and exact with his formula: "All in the state, nothing
outside the state." The state school is part and parcel of
the totalitarian whole, which above everything else depends
on putting a stop to freedom of speech. People are told
when and where and under what conditions to go to school,
exactly what to study, how to write novels, dramas and
poetry, what to say in the press, in movies and broadcasts,
and what to teach in biology and mathematics. Even when

they teach the commanded physics and mathematics, as we heard Korol quoting from *Pravda* in his work on Soviet education, teachers are under strict mandate to infiltrate: to force the one over-all regime on the children. "All in the state, nothing outside the state."

The point need not be labored, since, in spite of secret police, free peoples have been able to discover what makes a dictatorship "tick." In any such case, levelling has gone the limit, and the limit is the ideal.

The odd thing is that for some years we in America, taking so many freedoms for granted, thought little enough about the possible evils of Communist dictatorship. In American universities, a sprinkling of professors and students, no doubt a little confused or desperate and romantic, fell in line. Though we are a practical people, we did not so much as think about the most practical of problems. At best, we were young and green and therefore thoughtless. One recalls that illustrated works were published on a famous and in many ways excellent public school system in a Massachusetts city: and on the walls of schools, surely enough, was the photo of Stalin looking down benignly on teachers and students and telling them which way to go. It took shock treatments to wake us up so that we began to see what was going on and to understand that ideas and practices have consequences.

We mention these extreme matters to emphasize the fact that levelling can go too far, even under the guise of democracy, and to say that those who refuse an absolute levelling, in schools, in housing, in medicine, in religion, in economics and communications, have a point. The other side of the coin is that among us some of the levellers have not yet perfectly seen the point nor what is logically and patriotically to be done about it. Take the simple instance of levelling in American schools. Here the notion with a few rather self-appointed leaders and some followers whom we can only think sheepish is that, because of some fiat out of heaven, or a constitutional fiat, or the danger of allowing freedom, we ought to restrain the private, non-state school in America. Of course, we make and should make it toe the line of acceptable education for citizenship. But we are also likely to keep it uncomfortable and to keep making things difficult for it. Some of our good people seem to be unwilling in this case to allow freedom. They declare for freedoms and no doubt are sincere, but in their confusion they seem to be afraid of a genuine wide-open freedom in education. Free enterprise in other matters, but in education state enterprise only.

We remark at this point and shall later expand the remark that this un-American feeling against freedom in schools has various sources. In some persons and groups such as the POAU, it is part of an over-all war on Catholics; the alleged patriotic motif is a façade. In others, it arises from a sincere confusion combined with ignorance of history and the Constitution. In still others, as we have said, it comes from a drive to secularize everything.

For all those who believe in freedom of education, the present chapter is superfluous, since the chapter is written in defense of freedom and against the view of those tending to disallow freedom for establishing and maintaining private schools. We should be happy, of course, to learn that our argument here is mere valiant tilting against a straw man. But we believe that it is not: there is quite an animus worked up in some citizens and some educators against freedom for private schools. We scarcely need to say that, for better or for worse, the experience and sympathy of mankind have been with private schools, and this has been the case in both the Occident and the Orient.

As to the private schools' existence now in America, there are two main problems. One is the problem of finance, which is important though a secondary problem. This problem is how private schools can exist or so much as subsist. The California Federation of Labor, commenting on the contribution of Catholic schools to the state, has said: "The economic aspects of this contribution are staggering." Private schools even on the higher levels can rarely finance themselves. Some wealthy men and corporations contribute generously, but they do this irregularly, and they will help only such and such schools, and only in times of plenty; and so far as the state directly helps the schools, as it certainly does, these then might seem to lose something of their private character. The result is that private schools look as if they were living on borrowed time, and we may be sure that some of them are. It is no wonder that some of their leaders fight, e.g., in the voters' battle in New Jersey in 1959, to see that state colleges are not advantaged out of all proportion and to the destruction of private colleges.

That serious problem of financing is outside our problem which is the basic educational and ethical problem. Here, Americans must face the question of rights and freedoms and the good of persons and the general social good. The problem is clear when one sums up the case against private schools. This is rarely put in explicit terms. It is scarcely thought out, but it is felt, and, as Robert Bruère said as regards matters legally decided in the Nebraska one-language law and the Oregon public-schools-only law, it is strongly felt. It is an "animus." At the same time, it gives rise to situations such as those involved in those famous cases, and in the course of the debate it always becomes clear that the logic of the animus comes to something very simple. It comes to this: "We don't like you, and we would like to put a stop to your growth and, here and now, to your schools." That in fact is just what a state senator of Oregon said in 1958; he said that the aim of those arguing against the law that allowed free textbooks to Oregon private schools was to destroy those schools.

The words explicitly used for some years to shore up the case against private schools were "divided allegiance." At present, the popular and sharper word "divisive" is used, but of course the argument is the same and expresses the same feeling. It happens that Catholic primary and secondary schools form the great bulk of private schools on those levels, and the feeling is directed mainly but not wholly against them.

When Dr. James B. Conant, then president of Harvard, said in 1952 that we should close all private high schools, "smoke them out," the content of his speech as it appeared in *Vital Speeches* showed that he was against private schools for two reasons, and we may suppose that he was against some for one reason and against others for the other. He opposed private high schools of either a "religious" or a "financial" kind. Which suggests that he opposed some precisely because they were religious and other precisely because they were snobbish. But the word he used in putting together all private high schools and volunteering to be the leader in closing them was "divisive."

The report by Benjamin Fine in the *New York Times* was threefold: that in discussion Dr. Conant did use the words, "smoke them out," that he brought the question "out into the open," and that his large audience, educationists then assembled in Boston, went enthusiastically with him. What Dr. Conant really brought out into the open, we must remark even to the fair-minded Mr. Fine, was not a question. It was a feeling, the "animus" which Robert Bruère alleged is age-rooted in our people. Dr. Conant's vigorous declaration, the main part of which was published, made history, since this was probably the first time that any one educationally high-placed had declared, for whatever reasons, against the freedom of Americans to found and operate private schools.* It is one thing, not a very comforting one, to be sure, for some voters in the hinterlands to feel and say that they are dead-set against their neighbors' freedoms, and quite another and more ominous thing for like feelings and statements to issue from the mouth of a man in a high position.

We shall insist that the question, though it is a legal and constitutional one, is fundamentally an ethical question. What the "anti" position says is that private schools are an evil thing. For surely no one wants to smoke out and destroy what is good.

In itself, the question is relatively simple. It is a question of rights and freedoms. People want such and such types of schools, such and such types of teachers and of teaching, and that might seem, to the lover of freedom, to be those people's business and the end of the matter. In practice, it is far less simple. Given our ages-old pro and con feelings on this and a hundred subjects, such a question becomes complicated and cannot be written off with a gesture.

Let us say, too, that only part of the difficulty is this confirmed fear of our neighbors' freedom. Part of the difficulty in the whole educational situation lies in our lack of great leadership, a lack of leaders who, if they existed, would not have stood, even pre-sputnik, for educational

---

* The feeling for public schools only was strong in "Public Education and the Future of America," a sort of follow-up booklet issued by the Educational Policies Commission of the N.E.A. (1955). The booklet was evidently written by people who were far from being great leaders and who assumed that democracy needs what it called "universal public-school education."

infantilism * or for effective opposition, at least in high places, to academic freedom and the right to private schools. As I write these words, the head of the education department at a nearby state university has just been telling local public-school teachers that American education is superior to European. His thesis may or may not be sound; his proferred evidence for it was in three parts: a) that our children go much longer to school, b) that far bigger numbers and percentages of them enter "the university," and c) that a French educator told him how grieved is many a French child on being told, and perhaps unfairly, that he is officially dissuaded from trying to go on to higher levels. The naiveté of some people high in American "education" is what people used to call "a caution." It is evident that we need leaders. We even feel that we should be scolding heaven for not providing them; we are like Charlemagne when he asked Alcuin why the Kingdom did not have a dozen Jeromes and Augustines (and was told that the Lord gives us such men sparingly). Give us this day our daily bread. Give us, at least now and then, an educational leader, a man of vast simple vision who would see what needs to be done and what an educational army such as ours could do and how it could do it.

Meantime, there are matters that a senior in a private or a public high school should know. One of these is that American schools were private at the outset and for the most part for a long time afterward, and that private

* No real educator living in these times could, even from the first, have failed to rate Dr. Bestor's work highly, in his *Wastelands* and his *Restoration*. To effectuate "basic education" is what the times demand, even more than to effectuate religious or scientific literacy. Rear Admiral Rickover's striking work on *Education and Freedom* also accuses our schools of "educational infantilism." (We used the words in print some years ago.)

schools on all levels have been a distinctive mark of American life for over three hundred years. Also the child finishing high school should know, and, if not indoctrinated, probably as a rule does know, that famous topflight leaders in American democracy have been products of private schools; for example, Washington, Jefferson, Lincoln, the Roosevelts. In those notable instances, private education ran like this:

Washington was taught by the church-sexton and afterwards by what probably was an itinerant schoolmaster; finally, in mathematics and surveying by himself.

Jefferson "was well educated in small private schools"; then in a private college (William and Mary); and then in a private law office.

Lincoln was taught by his mother and his step-mother; less than one year by an itinerant schoolmaster or two, and finally by himself in a school as private as the fire in a log cabin "with no help except from borrowed books."

Theodore Roosevelt was taught by private tutors, and later at Harvard; and Franklin Delano Roosevelt was taught at two private schools: Groton and Harvard.

When we call the roster of our great patriots, heroes and leaders we find that quite a few of them and probably to date a big majority have attended private schools only. The results were satisfactory. Perhaps Jefferson, who himself saw the necessity of public education, would have had a better grasp of democracy and a greater love of freedom if he had attended public schools only. But how is anyone to prove this? The fact is that he attended private schools only.

The moral would seem to be that if more education was private and if far more of it was far more homespun, we might get greater leadership in decisive places. As matters stand, in the educational field we get many excellent third-raters, but very few leaders.

The whole point is so simple and elementary that children can grasp it, and of course they would like to grasp it, since they love all truth. Attendance at American private schools was sufficient on the school's part to create some of the foremost leaders yet known to democracy, the Washingtons, the Jeffersons, the Lincolns, the Roosevelts, and so on. It seems to us that the type of school that was good enough to do the school's part toward developing the type of citizen named is good enough, as regards citizens' training, for any one at any time. We may suppose that such patriots and democrats were thus exposed in school to influences which could work in the direction of "divided allegiance" and "divisiveness." Yet we are left with the fact that, as regards training for citizenship, theirs were good and perhaps remarkably good schools.

We are also left with the bothersome human question, always a fundamental one, of whether the child's parents have any rights that in any way transcend the state, and the question of whether the child is fully prepared for human life if his school is able to prepare him only to be a citizen of the city of man.

Besides, if there is any considerable case for closing, or in one way or another making difficult, the private grade schools and high schools, there would appear to be a corresponding case for closing Harvard, Oberlin, Notre Dame, Fordham, Vassar, and all private colleges and universities. On the basis of snobbery, there may seem to ultra-democrats to be some reason for closing some of them. This is a real though perhaps not a sufficient ground. The other ground, alleged against private grade schools and high schools, exists here also, the ground of divided allegiance: Harvard makes the student devoted to the Crimson, and

Yale to Old Eli, and Notre Dame and Oberlin perpetually invite the student to love the school and the church. O Unity, what anti-liberty crimes are committed in thy name!

We have been suggesting that persons and groups holding against private schools, on whatever level, have missed an elementary lesson in American history. That is less than half the story. More important is the fact that they misconceive democracy and misunderstand all forms of good government. They fail on the principle of "unity in diversity," a principle not less essential to good monarchy than to good democracy. We proceed to this fundamental aspect of the question.

Every one is acquainted with instances of unity in diversity. Husband and wife are an obvious instance. No matter how great the unity, the husband is necessarily himself and the wife is just as distinctly herself; the unity which is real does not destroy diversity, but serves to demonstrate it. Each continues life in terms of his or her mysterious identity. Unity in diversity is the only kind of unity people can have in marriage; and it is a good and sufficient kind, seemingly within the economy and purpose of the universe. The greatest lovers in the world can achieve unity only in diversity. If a man had to wait till he found a woman perfectly one with him in tastes and interests and being, he would wait a long time for a wife.

Much the same must be said regarding the good though qualified unity of child and parent, of mother and the child in her womb, of child and child in the family. Such unity remains unity in diversity; neither diversity nor unity is lost in favor of the other.

Though these matters are platitudinous, the real and growing need to assert them is evident in American society and generally throughout the Occident. In the Orient, too, at least China is invaded and conquered by this war of an exaggerated unity forced on diversity and on freedoms and rights. In our own country we encounter perfectly well-intentioned zealots who assume that democracy is merely another form of "line up, or else" autocracy.

The great threat to man today is not in diversity. Far from it. The threat is in a forced and unnatural unity. It is the "line up, or else" threat which now for at least a long generation has been wiping out free diversity and attempting to reduce natural and good diversity to forced unity, and not only in politics, since of course the reduction is occurring also in business and education and scientific research. In many areas, we encounter the organization man on the loose.

Take other instances of unity in diversity which lie all around us. Take the case of man and man in any partnership, even of a man and his identical twin brother; or of white with black, of Jew with Gentile. We want unity and in important areas we are suffering for it, but as a rule we have too much good sense to look for unity through the destruction of any person or group and their natural rights and freedoms. Unity is never good if it is bought at the price of our natural diversity.

In each area just mentioned we allow radical and irreducible diversity. But "allow" is hardly the word. We recognize and honor the inevitable diversity and the accompanying freedoms.

It is a sin to keep expatiating on obvious matters. The trouble is that even in a free society there will always be some good but rigid-minded persons of the single-track variety. What these persons say, and at times they say it with threats and vigorously, comes to this: "Diversity is divisive and means dividedness. If some diversity, therefore no unity. If unity—and we all want unity—then no diversity can be allowed: no diversity in schools, in creeds, in economic systems, in dress, in entertainments." Unity in diversity, or diversity in unity, fails to appeal to minds of this rigid type. Their assumption is "the more conformity the better."

The classic theoretic treatment of political and other unity in diversity is in Aristotle's *Politics* (Book II), where the author, arguing against a radical communizing, "the proposed new order of society," shows that to disallow diversity would be to destroy the state. "The error of Socrates must be attributed to the false notion of unity from which he starts. Unity there must be both of the family and the state, but in some respects only." Any defensible state supposes and promotes unity in diversity, and diversity in unity. So Aristotle claims, and his insight here is an immortal one. It is the first line of defence against all dictators. Aristotle claims that to try to level all off, to iron out and obliterate diversity, the terrible thing that is said to lead sure-fire to a ruinous "divisiveness," is to try to destroy the state itself; and surely, he says, the good of the state is not that which destroys it, but that which preserves it.

Grant so much with Aristotle: that which preserves any good state is diversity, a unified, but not a destroyed diversity of schools (here a Christian believer in democracy transcends Aristotle), a diversity of occupations, of ideas and philosophies, and possibly of races and national origins. If that is so for any good state, this same diversity is even more the life blood of the democratic state. As Francis Biddle says in *The Fear of Freedom:* "The democratic faith is the hardest faith there is," since it is "opposed to fanaticism, based on compromise, turned toward tolerance, welcoming variety and diversity." It is not a question of tolerating diversity as if it were the lesser evil, but of welcoming * it as a good and necessary ingredient of the democratic life and faith, and of course it is not only in America or in democracies that we need to respect diversity in unity.

The very genius of democracy is a genius for diversity in unity, for making one world out of many heterogeneous elements. *E pluribus unum* has a wide and varied application. As we all know too well, the whole-hog totalitarian regimes cannot put up with diversity, but demand a monolithic unity at any cost. Private schools are at once swallowed up; it is obvious that dictators must have public schools only. Any democratic nation always has an honorable place for private schools: Canada, Holland, England, France, pre-Hitler Germany. No dictator's nation has any place for them. One of the first things grabbed up by the omnicompetent state is the school. No private press, no private communications, no private schools; no privacy, no freedoms, all in the state, nothing outside the state. After Dr. Conant had spoken against the private high school and T. V. Smith had dutifully echoed him, James A. Pike (then at the Cathedral of St. John the Divine, New York City) remarked that the thought expressed by these men was totalitarian and would, if it had its way, impose a "monolithic educational philosophy" on the youth of America. Dr. Pike continued:

> In both cases the assault was made in the name of democracy, when in fact what these people stand for is one of the greatest threats to democracy . . . The first thing that the totalitarian rulers try to do is to destroy

* Mere "toleration" of the freedom of our fellow citizens is an insult, and we were sorry to see the idea of mere "toleration" worked so hard in *Religion in America*, "original essays on religion in a free society," ed. by John Cogley. New York, 1958.

any competitive educational systems which would provide the student an outlook which transcends the state and the aims of its leaders.

Democracy is not some state-controlled common philosophy and ethic which avoids "divisiveness"; democracy is the freedom to have one's own fundamental beliefs and to communicate them to one's children in the most effective way possible. Democracy is the freedom to be divided by fundamental beliefs and the privilege to seek to persuade others of their truth.

Democracy is not conformity; it is the privilege of non-conformity. The independent schools pre-date the state-controlled schools here and in England, and their existence preserves the essential pluralism of our culture. Their existence is as much a part of American life and philosophy as the more recently developed state system.

Whatever of the issue of religion in the schools, said Dr. Pike, democracy includes the freedom to provide private schooling for one's children. Obviously, such private schools are in a real sense "divisive," but so in a real sense are private churches, private houses and ownership and private wives and children. Any good society expects and accepts some privacy.

We must insist briefly on two points. First, private schools like anything private—private wives, private business—are divisive. That is undoubtedly and necessarily the case. To have diversity within unity, each to some degree managed and alleviated by the other, is the ideal and, in our country at least, is always being for the most part satisfactorily achieved. The dangerously divisive is something else. This could tear society apart. Yet any mature and balanced person knows that society has to run the chance of some real "divisiveness" if society is to allow freedom. It must run the chance of allowing private schools, private business, private scientific experimentation, private ownership and operation of steel plants, and of buses and airplanes. This is the chance we take when we allow freedom. There is a way to avoid the danger of divisiveness, and to avoid it at the source. The way to do it is to avoid freedom.

The other point, of relevance in a democracy and in a highly pluralistic society, is that leaders must continually work for unity in society. If schools of one kind or another, on a religious, an economic, or a snobbish basis, are tending to disrupt needed unity, as good citizens we have to see what is to be done. And so of other institutions such as money, religions, and universities. We are not so silly as to be levellers and naive egalitarians. But we cannot bless disrupters, either. It is especially important that members of differing religious faiths learn through practice to work together, and sometimes they succeed in doing so. We often repeat that nature will not suffer a psychological vacuum between groups, but will keep filling in the vacuum with guesses, suspicions, misunderstandings, and even with hate, conflict and war. What should fill the gap is friendship —between white and colored, Catholic and Protestant, Jew and non-Jew, East and West, capital and labor. Throughout the nation we observe many grass-roots attempts to smash these unnatural walls. In the Boston area some clergymen of various faiths have worked together for the last several years, and the idea is spreading to all of southern New England. In my own neighborhood, some priests and rabbis and ministers have met once a month for more than ten years to consider common problems. We are not an action group, but, in Newman's minimal formula, we are trying "to understand each other and allow for each other." Also in just this area as many as five hundred women of the three major faiths have been collaborating with what seems in effect to be much the same purpose. The finest achievement we have seen in the direction of unity in diversity is also in our neighborhood. A group of women have a "Catholic Action" unit on an entirely integrated basis, and its success, which is considerable, depends on two great principles: they meet in each other's houses and thus on a common social level, and they do not meet to study the racial problem, but some problem outside the tension area and yet common to all.

We could hardly have too much unity if we protect freedom and natural and highly desirable diversity. Or we could turn the terms around, and put "diversity" first. The "pluralist" idea has a natural place in a free country and in any democracy.

Experts say that essential to democracy is the two-party system. But such a multiple system is not peculiar to or limited to the political. We need to keep the way open to the "pluralist" view and practice in education, in faiths, in philosophies, economies and throughout our life in society.* All in the state, nothing not swallowed up by the state—that is the major twentieth-century heresy.

As part of his preparation and credentials for writing this book, the present writer is happy to have spent some of his time over the last ten or twelve years working with Jews and Protestants and secularists in espousing common causes and in helping to break down walls. He is happy to have many friends in each of the four major faiths of America, Jewish, Catholic, Protestant and secular, and also in the "fringe" religious groups; and to have friends among various occupational groups, farmers and miners and indus-

---

* See Jacques Maritain's "The Pluralist Principle in Democracy" and "The Possibilities of Cooperation in a Divided World," in *The Social and Political Philosophy of Jacques Maritain*, edited by Joseph W. Evans and Leo R. Ward. New York: Scribner's, 1955; pp. 116-130.

trial workers and lawyers and artists and professors. He is an active member of the National Council of Christians and Jews on both the local and the national level. He is a Catholic priest, and one of his best friends is a Mennonite minister's wife who has spent half her time for some years in an iron lung, praying and composing verse. He has given small parts of his vacations visiting in the homes of each of three Protestant ministers, partly to learn, though chiefly out of friendship. He is sure (with four popes from 1917 until today: no fear, then, that he'll shock Catholics) that mankind is one under God and was never meant to be torn and divided, in fact is meant for world community and world brotherhood. He has always supported the good things in his own neighborhood for brotherhood and unity. He is sure that in these affiliations he was backed by the Lord and by the late Pius XII, a man lauded for his belief in all mankind and his zealous charity and spirit of brotherhood toward all. At home in our own neighborhoods and our own nation we must work for unity and with unity. Nevertheless this must first and last be unity in diversity, and not flattened-out, levelled-down unity. In a democracy, people of many divergent faiths and of no faith, of differing philosophies, and espousing different economic and different educational systems live together and work together for the common good. Diversity in unity is the order of the day. One imposed creed, one imposed educational system, one imposed banking or medical system—in short the monolithic thing—is foreign to good government on any basis, as well as to freedom and democracy.

Is it really for the sake of democracy and for the sake of America that people would impose one educational system at any level? Not unless they are terribly misled and confused, and we remark in passing that at least Dr. Conant has been far from consistent in opposing private schools, since in fact he has often declared for diversity in unity. We are happy to invoke his fame on this, the American and democratic side of the question. To students graduating from Harvard in 1948 he said: "a wide diversity of beliefs and tolerance of this diversity has been the bedrock to which our national unity was anchored." Also in a volume of his published that year he said these memorable words * :

> For in a democracy with our traditions only those reasoned convictions which emerge from diversity of opinion can lead to that unity and national solidarity so essential to the welfare of our country . . . The significance of the independent institution is readily granted by even the most ardent supporter of tax-supported schools and colleges. No one would more regret their decline than those who themselves are laboring for the state-supported universities. The diversity of our educational pattern is as essential as diversity of opinion in this democracy of many creeds and conflicting political traditions.

Dr. Conant has nevertheless gone around in circles on pluralism *v.* monism in education. In his *Education and Liberty* he said that the greater the proportion attending private schools, "the greater the threat to our democratic unity."

If it is not for democracy and "undividedness" that people make direct or indirect war for public schools only, we have, as was said, to put it down either to ill-will or to confusion or to a drive for secularizing. Some of our zealous neighbors really want to fight something else, and the freedom to set up and conduct private schools and to send

* James B. Conant, *Education in a Divided World* (1948); pp. 193, 227.

children to them is, as we saw, an innocent victim caught in this trap. But of course there is at times that other source of the animus, namely an irreligious ideology and philosophy. Secularism naturally has little sympathy with anything like religion in schools or with anything done on a religious basis. How could it have? The freakish thing, however, as many have remarked, is that some serious religious groups, perhaps themselves feeling frustrated or fragmented and threatened, keep joining hands with secularism to carry on the fight against private schools. Such a stance is native to a Paul Blanshard whom we can only see as a sort of foreign growth in American society, an "anti" by trade, a man seemingly with little respect for freedom or for religion. But it is an odd stance for pious and professedly American and religious people.

In order to try to understand the total phenomenon, let us make a brief summary of secularist "musts" and "must nots" relative to teaching in American schools anything about God and faith and worship. Secularism in the schools is said to be a "must" because—

1. There is a constitutional and judicial declaration for secularism in schools. The Supreme Court is said to have decided it. A sort of steamroller on the subject has been Mrs. Agnes Meyer. The Court spoke and at that moment the question was closed. It was as simple as that for Mrs. Meyer. With some lack of assurance the Supreme Court had said that the method of teaching religion in public schools at Champaign, Illinois, represented too close a tie-in of church with state. Mrs. Meyer had no lack of assurance. Writing in the *Atlantic Monthly*, she said that Protestants must not buck or try to circumvent the decision —people have found interesting ways to do it—and Catholics, she said, must not hint that perhaps the question could in some way be reopened. *Roma locuta est.* What-

ever of the Court, Mrs. Meyer had spoken, and she is one of those vigorous citizens of good will who turn democratic decisions into dogmatic absolutes.

That is serious enough, since in her closed position we see that it is not merely the secularist but a believer of Mrs. Meyer's quality who is guilty of such translation. For all her goodness and zeal, and even because of these, Mrs. Meyer is representative of the type that metamorphoses democracy into a religion and commands everyone to line up; and such a person is all the more dangerous if ecstatic eloquence is combined with confusion. In the name of what she calls democracy, Mrs. Meyer throws her inquisition into high gear. Here is her own expression of some of her basic dogmas. "Democracy can generate a system of moral principles," she says, and these principles, which she discovers to be America's "secular morality," beget "a concept of democracy itself as a moral idea which unites all peoples, all religions, races and cultures." This moral idea, she declares, is "secularism rightly understood." She ends up with the rousing if somewhat shocking assertion that public education is "the American religion." *

Rough stuff, especially for believers in freedom and for all those innocent bystanders who had thought that man himself is not subject in all that he is to any political community: not totally subject, said Aquinas, to any non-transcendent power, but only to God. Once Mrs. Meyer has transformed democracy into an absolute and turned public education into a religion, man is out of luck. Man is absolutely subordinated to the state, and is not allowed to squirm. Here we meet the perfect type of those who absolutize the relative.

* See *The Commonweal,* 60 (June 4, 1954), pp. 212-213; and Agnes E. Meyer, "Are Our Public Schools Doing Their Job?" *Atlantic Monthly,* 188 (Febr. 1949).

2. A second confusion was cited in the preceding chapter. For a short while the McCollum decision seemed to freeze the Constitution into a secularist document, an historical development full of interest and novelty as well as of peril. But it is evident that such a decision by courts or by citizens is much more a secularist "must" than a rights-of-man or a constitutional "must." This confusion is effective with both the popular and the official mind, and it leads some innocent persons to suppose that the Constitution declares for what Justice Frankfurter has called the "absolute separation" of church and state. Misled by the well-known "wall of separation" and "a strong wall," probably a majority of teachers in public and private schools make the same simple supposition when they encounter the issue in their school work. Far more serious and really unpardonable is the fact, already noted, that several justices on the Supreme Bench have evidently been subject to this "absolute separation" confusion. The common confusion leaves citizens and justices zealously guarding a non-existent wall.

The condition amounts at last to a sort of obession and fosters the myth that the Constitution does after all somewhere declare for secularism. Unfortunately the myth affects persons who are far from being secularist in belief or practice. These people suffer a schizophrenic split between what, in spite of the Zorach decision, they take to be a constitutional secularism, promulgated by judicial decrees, and a secularism which they would not want at all: secularism in the family, the Church, and the universe. Since the Constitution is thought to be secularist, in their minds the national life is secularist in an official way, and so are public schools.

Such a condition is less unpalatable to Protestants than to Catholics. Since Luther's day, Protestants have been, as many observers have remarked, somewhat attuned to the idea of a "wall" between religion and social realities. They have tended to erect a wall between the Bible, faith and worship on the one hand, and education, culture, law, economics and politics on the other. Such an obstruction is radically unsatisfactory and will not do in any area for Protestants, Catholics or Jews.

3. There is an anti-Catholic declaration for secularism in schools. We like to suppose that this is effective in relatively few, and generally only in those without basic education in things religious or American. Writing in *Commentary* (November, 1952), Will Herberg said that it was taken for granted at first that the public schools were to be non-sectarian Protestant, but Jews and Catholics soon began to be legion among students, teachers and school administrators. The spirit of public education today, Mr. Herberg said,

> is, by and large, secularist, even militantly so. (I use the term to signify an outlook on life in which man is held to be sufficient unto himself and God disappears as an unnecessary, outmoded concept.) The most influential educational philosophies and centers of teachers' training are self-consciously secularist, and so is educational practice in almost every part of the country . . . many important Protestant leaders are deeply concerned, even alarmed. This concern, however, has resulted in very little, in part because of a confusion of counsel, but primarily because Protestant concern about the schools has been thoroughly bedeviled by the all-absorbing preoccupation with the Catholic "menace" . . . Practically every Protestant leader with whom I discussed the matter referred in vague but disturbed terms to the "ominous growth" of the Catholic Church in this country.

Mr. Herberg, who returned in 1957 to this and related subjects, says that he has discovered the sort of undercover logic which we earlier suggested: Catholics have done something to build and man schools which in design are free of secularism. One does not like Catholics, feels that at bottom and by prescription this is a Protestant country, fears Catholic growth and Catholic power. One is therefore in general against freedom for Catholics.* Therefore, secularize all schools. We know that this simple logic, once it is brought out into the open, convinces few, and we hope that in time hardly anyone will accept it. Meantime, such a logic-devouring man as Paul Blanshard thrives on this "anti" feeling, and so do those who line up with him.

4. There is an anti-divisive and presumably pro-unity declaration for secularism. As we saw, the anti-divisive feeling at times assumes a degree of unity neither desirable nor possible within any social and political body and intolerable in a democracy; it demands too much of a good thing, and if let go, the feeling does harm to democracy and education. We also saw that Dr. Conant's lively speech for monolithic unity in education was in a way fortunate; it served to bring the fundamental wrongness of this feeling out into the open.

5. There is a pure and simple declaration for secularism. Some people want secularism, in schools and everywhere, and want it because they think it is the truth of things. This can be a straightforward secularism, not claiming to be something else, such as savior of freedom or America. It can be exactly what it is—secularism, nothing better or worse. It may at times be mild or have any degree of belligerency. Late in the forties Roy Wood Sellars, then at Michigan University, asked: "Could religion, as a concern for man's existence and the human situation, shift from the perspective of super-naturalism to that of naturalism?"

* The same sort of logic is one of the reasons why people are against Jews.

Given Dr. Sellars' meaning of terms, this is a fair question. Could religion take "a naturalistic world view as a background?" He merely wanted to know whether, in justice to data, we might drop reference to any transcendent God or gods and understand everything in naturalistic terms, in purely humanitarian and non-transcendent terms. Confused persons try to make secularism mean democracy and the unity of mankind, but Dr. Sellars' question is as direct and fair as sunshine, and it is the basic philosophical question. Such a question has nothing specious or opportunist about it and merely wants to know what we are to think about naturalistic secularism as the total and final answer.

6. There is a "democracy demands it" and "science demands it" declaration for secularism. This rhetorical type of appeal was much used by the older prophets such as H. G. Wells, John Dewey, Julian Huxley and T. V. Smith, and for at least a generation "democracy" and "science" were combined into the feeling that "progress demands it." A "humanist" manifesto, emerging from the first secularist international, illustrates this nineteenth century secularism. From six nations, people were assembled in Amsterdam a few years ago for that first secularist international. They heard Julian Huxley talk on "evolutionary naturalism," and under this heading he said he was outlining a creed according to which man can carry the process of evolution to new levels.

Mr. Huxley, who more recently carried his program to the Orient, declared at Amsterdam: "If men believe that the right development of natural and human resources is the nearest we can come to absolute destiny for our species collectively and individually, this will spell a fundamental change in the social and political outlook . . . Population control becomes an immediate aim and eugenics a long term goal, both of them central for political thought and action." The group repeated the "democracy, science, and progress" declaration for secularism. The following were the stated objectives. First, the fullest possible development of every human being. Second, worldwide application of scientific methods to problems of human welfare. Third, the greatest possible freedom of individual development compatible with the rights of others. Fourth, utilizing, for the purposes of peace, the new power which science has given us.

7. There is a "wave the flag" and "America first" declaration for secularism. This is the vigilante and watchdog type of secularism, and is one of the more primitive forms of secularistic faith.

8. There is "the churches precipitate it" declaration for secularism. The churchmen are far from agreement and sometimes their tactics look like those of free enterprise merchants out for trade. Leaders of each faith at times even malign members of other faiths. In short, certain leaders of religion appear to be more "anti other" than co-religionist lovers of God and man. From this lively and almost too free scene some observers conclude to secularism for schools and society. It was because of this type of internecine struggle among Protestant churches that Horace Mann advocated the ousting of sectarian Protestant "non-Biblical" religion from public schools.

Secularism is not born full grown, but naturally proceeds by degrees and areas. The religious person innocently assumes that nothing is purely secular and that interstellar spaces as well as the realms of person and society declare the glory of God. Because in his view all things fall within a providential order, nothing can be totally senseless and meaningless. Then some day he wakes up to discover how secularized his own society really is. He sees much business activity seemingly drained as dry of reference to good and evil, let alone to the transcendent God, as the most zealous secularist could wish.* Then he sees that political activity in some of its big powers, inside and outside Russia, has the look of being Machiavellian and secular, since it tends to be guided by expediency. He notices that many a war, so far as its kingpins are concerned, is secularized, and also the precarious peace; and so perhaps of art and entertainment and sciences and sex and marriage and family life and education.

All of which approaches an actual secularism and not a secularism by ideological or legal fiat. Besides, we may suppose that some men at last become "connatured" to secularism and begin to believe it true because they have long lived it.

By its own nature "secularism" has to assume that man lives in a world that radically has no "meaning," a world that is not directed by any mind toward any good end. The world has to be taken to be a meaningless colossus that happens to be going along. During the eternal and meaningless gyrations of whatever is, life automatically appeared; then brute-animal life, and then human-animal life. In this meaningless constellation of things, man is a break in the continuity—and yet he has no right to upset it. He is an oddity. He imposes direction and order on himself and on things, and at one look sees all time and space and all being. He acts with freedom and a kind of divining intelligence. This means that he is a person. But in a simple secularist view, man is the only orderer and the only person in a universe which, until he arrived, was totally impersonal. That is the secularist view expressed so

* Or so it has often appeared and is ordinarily thought. And yet just at the present time, some corporations hold costly and elaborate conferences on the ethical problems incident to business.

consistently in Bertrand Russell's *A Free Man's Worship*. The conclusion of Russell, who (as Sir Frederick Pollock remarked) likes to be a kind of bad boy, is an exhortation to love your neighbor, since you and he are in the same sinking boat. The secularist gospel is radically pessimistic, and in Communist secularism, trying to go against what it takes to be the grain of the universe, it remains pessimistic.

The believer, as also the merely practical secularist, is shocked when he sees what is implied in the Communist or other secularization of society. What it comes to is Russell's or any secularist's gospel. If sex, the family and the home are secularized; if banking, industry and ownership are secularized, and with them such activities as education and war and peace and art and science, we are reduced to a "man, lord of the world" philosophy. H. G. Wells preached such a gospel, and quite consistently died in despair. On the secularist view, up to now nothing is —or at any rate, nothing is known to be—more ultimate in being, knowledge and goodness than man. Then apparently the best a man could do, since he is inevitably a worshipping animal, would be, in Bertrand Russell's words, to "worship at the shrine that his own hands have built." The best he could do would be either to worship himself or to worship mass power in some form or other. In short, secularism is not an "out" for such a man; it is a report of where he is. The secularist is more cornered than is the man of "the old time religion."

In Western society where men are threatened not only by Communism but by the pessimistic views of non-Communist secularism, religious education has an immense work to do. We have passed out of the Dewey and Wells age of easy secularist optimism into the Sartre age of secularist despair. It is no longer possible for us to presume, as White-head for instance did almost of right presume, a simple and magnificent benevolence. In face of our more difficult situation, we need many things and among them a fully religious education both in homes and schools. We need to have at least some boys and girls receiving an education in full-length Christian liberal culture such as is best out-lined by Christopher Dawson,* and such a religious and liberal education as presumably could be made available in our present Catholic and Lutheran schools, primary and secondary, in Jewish primary schools, and in church-re-lated colleges and universities. We need some such edu-cation made available far more widely, but for the present let us enter a claim for it at least to that extent.

That education is in various degrees made available now in the types of schools just enumerated. But those church-related schools and colleges and universities must be made and kept first-rate in all senses, at no matter what cost and sacrifice, and they must have at least the moral backing of all who believe in America and all who make any pre-tense to believing in mankind. More is at stake than apologetic and propaganda ends for some particular reli-gion. To encourage religious education, in and out of schools, might of course help particular religions and also help all religions. That would perhaps be a result and by-product. The aim would be the good of the child and the nation, and of mankind, too, since today we must think beyond our own isolated national and Western good.

That is one side of the picture. The child needs this education and at least the nation needs the shock effect of it. The other side is that it has become extremely diffi-cult for us, and also for its exponents, to conceive that

* Dawson's plan is stated in our last chapter.

modern any more than ancient secularized education can do what needs to be done in order to understand man, to free him and to afford him techniques for the progressive conquest of freedom. Here we speak of education in schools and homes and movies and television programs, fixed or otherwise. The major lesson afforded us by the twentieth century interest in history and its meaning is this dual lesson: a) that man is inevitably a religious animal, and b) that religion among all peoples is public, its rituals and ceremonies the main public event, the most interesting and commanding in peoples' lives. For our schools to run away from this worldwide lesson is to refuse to learn. And in the circumstances of today's life in America, to try remanding religion totally to the somewhat disestablished home or to the individual conscience would be both unrealistic and unscientific in relation to the kind of thing religion is. It would be unfair, besides, to the child and unheedful of the most notable contemporary studies in humanity.

The executive director of the Oak Ridge Institute of Nuclear Physics is an Episcopalian priest, the Reverend William G. Pollard, who was trained first as a physicist. Dr. Pollard thinks on the present matter as we do. This is what he says [*]: "The real trouble with the academic community, as I sense it, is that it hasn't any resources with which to carry on . . . Individuals do have resources to cope with what it faces today. There is a sort of sense of despair, of fragmentation, of not knowing where to go or what to do."

If any such thing as even a ghost of despair is occurring, it is not something for either a believer or a secularist-believer to welcome as a kind of savior, though a Com-

---

[*] William G. Pollard, in *The Christian Idea in Education*. Ed. by Edmund Fuller. Yale Univ. Press, 1957; pp. 29-30.

munist might hail it as a possible opening wedge. Such despair would mean the loss of something vital and fundamental, and we cannot see that it would mean the gain of anything. People need the nerve to live. The old academic community in America, say for the past two generations, was something to be proud of in many ways. At least on the higher levels in both the private and the state universities, it was almost too sure of itself, some of its citizens aloof from reality, aristocratic and prudish; and some of them still are irredeemable romantics. Its extrovert members, and those won the day, looked to and rejoiced in progress, scientific research and achievement; and in social matters, it thrived on a kind of liberal humanitarianism as well as a fecund academic freedom.* In its public avowals, that community was becoming secular on the part of both faculty and administration, and down to our day it is a little exhilarating and a little shocking when the president of even a private university such as Harvard makes official statements on the side of religion. We had almost reached the stage of assuming that a university president has no such freedom, and this because we assumed that a university is, quite contrary to Newman's well-known thesis, of its nature secular. A man highly placed in university administration might be deeply religious in conviction and practice, but that fact was supposed never to show through in his official academic life. The president was supposed either to keep mum or to show himself secular. The history and psychology of religion might be taught, so long as all parties by a sort of tacit consent avoided theology.

* According to Hofstadter and Metzger (*The Development of Academic Freedom in the United States*, New York: Columbia University Press, 1955; pp. 196-201), academic freedom, especially in science, was notable in America even in the eighteenth century.

Things are changing, though not generally or all of a sudden. Our business now in American academic life on all levels is to seek goals that at least are different. The more strenuous times and a more scientific spirit and habit will not let us bypass religion and theology in universities. The earlier neutral attitude might do when the gods threw everything into our lap. At least it might seem to do. But today a mere neutral and secular learning is inadequate both to reality and to the crisis. Today the academic community needs a shot in the arm, and this can come to it only from some higher sense of meaning and purpose. On this point we are happy to have confirmation from words of Clarence H. Faust * who has said that the root of recent difficulties in American education has been "the loss of a religious tradition which provided a rationale and gave richness to the subjects commonly taught—reading, writing, arithmetic, geography, and history." Dr. Faust says that the need as things stand is "to lay the base for a sufficiently full and comprehensive public philosophy," and he is aware that in this regard we are far more in the problem stage than obviously nearing a solution.

* Clarence H. Faust, *Toward Understanding American Education*. Yellow Springs, Ohio: Antioch Press, 1957; pp. 17, 27.

CHAPTER 5

Judeo-Christian Insights

Jews and Christians lay claim to sources of knowledge not at once available to others. This knowledge, based on the Bible, is systematized in their respective theologies. The problem of a generalized Judeo-Christian learning is the problem of whether there is available to Jews and/or to Christians any non-theological knowledge not at once available to others.

This old and much neglected problem must be considered, and for several good reasons. First, because if any such learning is possible or actual, we would like to know what it is, and what it is like, so that we could identify it or even on occasion seek it. Secondly, because if any such thing exists, we Americans and our forbears in Europe have been exposed to it for centuries, it is deep in our attitudes and assumptions, and nobody could understand us without understanding this world of thought, and action affected by thought, within which we have so long moved. Thirdly, because if there has really been any such thing, then presumably we have lived it and in that way have become "connatured" to it, and, as an object to be learned, it has become "congenial" to us and the "connaturing" has worked both ways, we to it and it to us. For centuries, no matter what its truth and adequacy, this learning must have fit us like an old shoe or an old hat; we have long been right at home in it. In that case, we would have scarcely noticed it, and long before America was born, its assumptions would have been worked into our bones, and these assumptions sat in with our Founding Fathers and cast a deciding vote. Lastly, if we are to learn at all regarding religion in American schools, we may be well advised to begin close to home.

Let us see how we are to take this alleged thing, a Judeo-Christian learning, to which we shall affix the modifier "Christian," for the sake of simplicity and also because the "thing" is thus more "connatured" to more of us.

A minor thesis of the chapter will be that it is time for men of learning, whatever their faith or scepticism, to begin to catch up with the question of whether there possibly is such a thing as a Christian learning, a Christian scholar, a Christian school or college. The question is as old as St. Augustine; it received a notable formulation in St. Anselm; a positive reply to it was stock in trade for centuries, and it has been newly bruited for two generations. We are asking scholars to catch up; if need be to shed inhibitions and proceed to honor themselves and their profession by considering the question.

We know that we are asking something difficult. For apologetic reasons, Christians—and perhaps liberal Jews— have long shied away from the very question of a "Christian learning" and a "Christian philosophy." The reaction to the question by a famous Catholic scholar at a famous non-Catholic American university is representative. He was flabbergasted that anyone should raise the question and in effect said: "Well, if there is any such thing as Christian learning, I could think of many scholars who would be shocked to find it out." *

Let us begin with what by a tour de force may be called John Dewey's reaction to the problem of a Judeo-Christian learning. A born pioneer and a man who in our opinion was radically a lover of man, Dewey did much to help to emancipate the American child's mind, and of course Dewey, himself a secularist in later life, was affected by the Christian climate in which he spent his youth and by the relatively Judeo-Christian climate in which he spent his adult life. A weakness in Dewey was his impatience with the slow processes of history and of exact studies. He worked fast and did not do things twice, and was impatient with criticism. Late in his life, he still threw his weight around; e.g., in an article in *Fortune* (August 1944), and in the introduction, newly done for the occasion, to his *Problems of Men* (1946). In those pieces he said that new philosophies and new theories of education were being expressed in America, and it was clear that he therefore thought them illegitimate and heterodox. In the *Fortune* article he used an incomparably good phrase to describe the thought of an age; the phrase was "medieval theological philosophy." According to Dewey, this theological philosophy held that "the basis of all ultimate moral principles" is in the supernatural, in what he called the "miraculously revealed and sustained." Perhaps this is just what the philosophy so well christened by Dewey should have done. It is another question whether the philosophy did any such thing.

Applied to the educational theory held by American

* Fear of the question shows through also in "What *is* the Aim of Catholic Education?" by Richard W. Rousseau, S.J., in *The Catholic World* (October, 1959); pp. 24-29.

Catholics, Dewey's implied criticism would have been a much better fit. ("Theological philosophy" makes sense too as a description of some non-Catholic positions, e.g., Reinhold Niebuhr's or Buber's.) Whatever of Protestant or Jewish education, Catholic educators both in America and abroad have yet to think their educational theory through from start to finish. Our own view of their theory as expressed in America is that it is inevitably inchoate. More important, it is as yet unaware of its own resources in the line of a positive and creative dynamism. Of course at this early date it is far from its rightful peak and is often misconceived and mistaken by Catholics.

With all due respect for the "Jewish learning" which preceded Christian learning and which should always accompany it, we must ask: What is this thing, "Christian learning"? What is "a Christian scholar"? Few pundits in Catholic or other schools free themselves sufficiently to ask the question. It is an obvious question, nevertheless, given the Christian background of education in America and given the immense American Catholic educational establishment and the impressive Jewish and Protestant educational establishments. All these are staring us in the face. We have firsthand experience of them, and as Dewey unforgettably said, "Experience asks questions." Do they have any being of their own? The experience of the fact is so big and so close to us that we are blinded by it. Fortunately some American Catholics are insisting on the question,* as

---

* The question was raised by Leo R. Ward's *Blueprint for a Catholic University*, St. Louis: Herder, 1949. More recently a sort of dialectical inquiry into the quality of Catholic learning in America, begun by John Tracy Ellis in "American Catholics and the Intellectual Life," *Thought*, 30 (Autumn 1955) (published in book form by Heritage Foundation, Chicago, 1956), has been continued by Gustave Weigel, "American Catholic Intellectualism," *Review of Politics*, 19 (July, 1957) and by Thomas F. O'Dea, *American Catholic Di-*

are a few Dutch Reform scholars. Few among Protestants in general have asked the question, "What is a Protestant learning or a Christian learning?" We do not know even one American Protestant who has come to anything like grips with the problem. A group of Evangelicals has made some study of "Christian education" though without coming to any precise terms.* The Hazen pamphlets, a continuing series, are justly famous, but again are a little too general and broad to come to terms with our question. † We would like to see exacting work done on the compound problem: a Christian scholar, a Christian school, and Judeo-Christian learning; and we would be pleased to see the best Jewish scholars collaborate. Criticism begins at home, and this chapter as well as this book claims to offer constructive criticism.

That is only the beginning of our story. Mankind is in the middle of an urgent situation. The fix we are in demands that at least an attempt be made to circumscribe the idea of "Christian" and "Judeo-Christian" as applied to learning and school and scholar. The author is thoroughly

---

lemma, New York: Sheed and Ward, 1958. Much more positive though yet critical works are Leo R. Ward's *New Life in Catholic Schools,* St. Louis: Herder, 1958, and Justus George Lawler's *Catholic Higher Education in Perspective,* Westminster, Md.: Newman, 1959.

* See *Christian Education in a Democracy.* Ed. by Frank E. Gaebelein. New York: Oxford University Press, 1951. Notable also are Nash's *The University in the Modern World,* Macmillan, 1944; Coleman's *The Task of the Christian in the University,* New York: Association Press, 1947; and Moberly's *Crisis in the University,* London, S.C.M. Press, fifth printing, 1952. Far the best cooperative effort of American Christians toward understanding Christian education is *The Christian Idea of Education,* ed. by Edmund Fuller, Yale University Press, 1957.

† Hazen Pamphlets are published by Hazen Foundation, 400 Prospect St., New Haven, 11, Conn. Among them we might cite G. K. Chalmers, "The Prerequisite of Christian Education," and Reinhold Niebuhr, "The Contribution of Religion to Cultural Unity."

committed to saying that we should have religion as a study somehow available in every American school. If we are to have it, the study will, in the main, be of the Christian and the Judeo-Christian understanding of man's relation to God. That goes without saying. However, the crux of the question as raised in this chapter is whether believing Jews and believing Christians have any non-theological learning available to them that is not equally and as immediately available to persons and groups not professing Jewish and Christian beliefs. The question has special difficulties in any case. But for American Protestants it is extraordinarily complex. This is because Protestantism in our country is so latitudinarian both in idea and in fact. Even so, Protestants, as well as Jews and Catholics, in effect keep answering the question: they do claim special insights. Concretely, the question goes like this: at least in social sciences, and again in philosophical studies on nature and man and God, what if anything can Christians or Jews know that others do not know or do not so readily know?

Our reply to the basic question may be put in the following way. It has made a vast difference to the matters held and taught, in areas such as those just mentioned, that the Bible exists and that Christ lived and died. This Bible-and-Christ body of teachings is so integrated with Western thinking and living that we naturally take it for granted. But notice the new intellectual activity aroused by the discovery (1947) of the Dead Sea Scrolls. On this subject, scores of scholarly and popular works have appeared almost overnight in all languages. We all have a hunch that, perusing the Scrolls, we will learn something precious not merely about some defunct monks, but about God and man and time and money and "the meaning of things." We all have a vague notion that those old monks had up their sleeve more than "this world's wisdom" even in regard to temporal and natural things. Why do we feel that way? Because we accept, even in spite of our professed theory, the idea of a Judeo-Christian learning. That is why all want to know more about how Jewish monks lived at the time of Christ. The Bible-and-Christ way of believing and living has profoundly influenced the content of what we claim naturally to know.

At the moment we are not concerned with the possible validity of any affirmed Judeo-Christian knowledge, but only with the fact that this special, non-theological knowledge is affirmed by Jews and Christians. The simple depth question asked by an old farmer and his wife after Hiroshima suggests the world of thought and conceivable knowledge within which even the untutored Christian moves. The question was this: "Do you think almighty God will let man destroy himself?" Daedalus might have made some sense out of that question, but he could scarcely have asked it. The farmer and his wife were one up on Daedalus because the Bible and Christ have made a difference to thought structures and to the lives of persons and societies. In formal and minimal terms, we are now in a different frame of reference. This has to make a difference to theory and to life. It has done so and it will continue doing so. To bring the source and cause to one word, the Gospel has played a part in revealing man to man and again in revealing nature, e.g., "nature" as created, to man. Few if any would think the Gospel insignificant in revealing God to man.

There is a vast difference between the Egyptian-Grecian-Roman world—all glamor and glory as it is—and the Jewish-Christian world, no matter how much the latter has adopted and adapted the former. Clement of Alexandria was a richly cultured soul, "perhaps of Athenian origin," but I think we have to say that even in his natural knowledge, for instance of good and evil and the meaning of "manners," he was at least one up on the greatest pagan Greeks. Even in grasping natural things, Clement had the advantage of a light that his pagan contemporaries did not have. In this respect, he was simply a Christian. Again, the Far East is great. But great or small, it has not generally had the Jewish-Christian world of understandings and consequent action. The differences between East and West are complex, but many of them may be referred to two roots. The root of the difference is the Bible and the Church. Take away the Bible and the Church, and in thought as well as in action and for good or for ill we still have the pagan world, civilized and uncivilized.

The difference first of all is in theory about man and nature and God, and secondly and inevitably in action. A faithful Jew or Christian cannot think at all points about man and nature and God as either an enlightened or unenlightened pagan does, and cannot act in all matters as a pagan does. We must at least admit that a pagan cannot fall as far as a Christian can. With modern equipment at hand and with a Christian world of understandings still ringing in his ears, the apostate and lapsed Christian makes the most successful despot. Or turn matters around. A pagan cannot think as a Christian does, nor act as a Christian does. In its thought and its action, a Christian society has some kind of being and some kind of meaning that a pagan society does not have. A Christian society must be itself, and a pagan society must be itself. It is correct to say that faith is the difference; but this way of stating it is incomplete. The issue involves more than faith—it involves knowledge.

We come back all the time squarely to one point. There is no use saying that a pagan does see or can see on all subjects as a Christian sees. In the early days of Christianity, a tension arose between the divine society and the temporal society; and this tension, says Christopher Dawson, must to some degree remain, and it can be beneficent.* So too for the tension within the Christian himself between natural learning and any supernatural and theological learning; it is a standing task for scholars to keep making one world of the two. So again for the tension in our society between men who know merely as pagans and men who do not know merely as pagans: some tension and misunderstanding is inevitable, and each party has to learn to make allowances. Here, above all, we meet the "pluralist" character of our society. This time, pluralism is demanded even within the individual, since any of us is more or less pagan and more or less Christian.

Of course, pagan and Christian agree on many points in many fields of learning. But pagan can scarcely be expected to be at one with Christian on all points of sociological theory for instance, or ethical theory, or political theory, or economic theory. This is merely saying that pagan cannot be Christian and that Christian cannot be pagan. Divergence is sure to occur on some fundamental points, and above all because of divergent views on man's origin, nature and destiny. Move any of those pegs even a little, and everything is changed. To cite what we have said elsewhere † :

What difference does it make? Quite a difference to philosophy, and to sociology, and to a man's or a community's or even a civilization's psychological grasp of things, of man, of good and evil, of "meaning" and "sense" in the universe, of nature itself. We are naive if

* See Christopher Dawson, *Understanding Europe.* New York: Sheed and Ward, 1952; pp. 20-21, 207.

† Leo R. Ward, *New Life in Catholic Schools.* St. Louis: Herder, 1958; pp. 43-44.

we think—and some Christians do think it—that God's word on things and on man makes no difference to what we know and to what we advisedly teach in sociology or in political science. The Christian knows some of these matters on theological grounds, and because he does, he and his civilization can outrun the pagan and his civilization in the chance to know them on psychological, sociological, and philosophical grounds, which in a way are the pagan's own grounds.

And so the difference begins in theology, and moves naturally into philosophy, and affects social sciences and the content of literature and the arts. It is easy to cite cases in point. It is evident that Aristotle, who taught Thomas Aquinas so much, does not claim to know some matters in philosophy that Thomas Aquinas claims to know. It is evident that the venerable Homer cannot express what Dante expresses. This is because he does not know some things that Dante claims to know. For the same reason, it would be difficult, to put it mildly, for a twentieth-century pagan with all of Homer's powers to express what Dante expresses. There is no use trying to reduce pagan to Christian, or pagan social theory to Christian social theory.

To see how important an understanding of "Christian learning" is, let us look briefly at the Catholic schools in America, at their origin and aims. This foray will give us a large indigenous instance, along with empirical materials, and then we can return to our fundamental inquiry into any possible "Christian learning."

As is well known, the Catholic schools in America were not set up primarily for intellectual purposes, but to save the faith and morals of boys and girls, harassed in mind and freedoms by Protestant teachers and teachings in professedly public schools. All the records show that this idea of saving faith and morals from Protestant invasion was effectively present and dominant, just as the idea of saving faith and morals from secular invasion is now present and dominant. To such an idea we must in passing pay three compliments. As an end and motive it was natural and necessary and to be expected in the circumstances, and is in fact an idea not lost sight of and not to be lost sight of by any church society at any time or by any political society when the latter is setting up schools. As Robert Drinan has said and as Justice Douglas implied in delivering the decision in the Zorach case, to promote the common good the state is obliged to promote many interests, including the interests of religion. Secondly, we may suppose that this defensive idea (soon mixed with the idea of propagating the faith) has been on the whole fairly effective, since although many Catholics and other students have lost their faith, * the Catholic population has continued to grow out of proportion to the growth of the total American population. This phenomenon, still occurring, is accounted for in part by the existence of Catholic schools. Thirdly, that immediately practical motive of saving faith and morals has fallen in admirably with the prevailing pragmatic temper (we await a competent study of the influence of pragmatism on American Catholics).

The question we raise at the moment is whether it is not high time to find a more properly academic end than "save the faith and morals" for Catholic schools and in general for church-related schools. Suppose we should say, reverting to a classic notion, that schools on any level are

---

* As already noted, G. K. Chalmers, in the chapter "To believe and to doubt well" in his *The Republic and the Person,* showed how intolerable, not to say inane, it is to expect college boys and girls just out of high school to be adroit sceptics and yet to keep their faith.

advisedly set up for an intellectual good and end. The question then would only be whether a directly intellectual end is a justifiable end of teaching and of school learning. Schools could serve other ends, and at any time schools do serve many other ends in society, and it is evident that during the whole time covered by Marrou's great work (1000 B.C. to 500 A.D.) they were serving political society.* They serve the church society, the political society and the family, and if any of them disserve any of these we must be ready to reform or close the schools. The implication is that schools, having much autonomy at least in America, are in many ways naturally subordinate to church and state and the family. They serve the economic life which in turn, though it needs freedom, has ends beyond itself. They serve many sciences which demand freedom if they are to thrive in the long run, though some of these sciences have on occasion to serve ends beyond themselves; e.g., to be subordinated to the three societies just mentioned; and it is evident that in our day physical and mathematical sciences are subordinated to the political good. As a discerning mind said on Hiroshima day, "That writes finis to scientific freedom." Political societies are using sciences to put satellites in orbit and to make war and peace. The schools also serve other less natural and inevitable societies, such as labor, military, and business organizations. Schools do not ordinarily set out to do any of this, but doing it is within the whole complex of things done in the society of which they are an intimate part.

The economic system has freedom and ends and a kind of being of its own. It has to have these, in order to live and breathe. In order to live and grow, science has to have

* H. I. Marrou, *A History of Education in Antiquity*, tr. by George Lamb. New York: Sheed and Ward, 1956.

freedom and a kind of self-end and self-being. Free, self-determining—and yet subordinated! That seems strange. But it is not strange if we know that there are ends within ends, and that man himself, to say nothing of economics and science, has a being belonging to him and freedoms and an end proper to him, and yet at the same time falls within a larger whole, of being and freedom and ends, to which he naturally belongs.

The school as an institution is not better than man and may be considered as worthy as science or the economic system. It has its freedoms, its being, its ends. But what is its proper end? Let us say that it has as primary and direct end to help open up the minds of youths, to help them begin to see a world of good—if that is what the world is—and of beauty and truth. This end, viz., knowing things, is not the end of the universe, but it is an end that the universe would like to promote, since man, a part of the given universe, naturally desires to know. Maintained historically among many peoples and in many different ways, the school tries to help nature do this work which nature wants to do.

John Dewey has the magnificent formula that the end of society in general is to give to every man the chance to grow to the full stature of his possibilities.* Sometimes Dewey vigorously denies ends for schools or anything else, but here, it seems to us, his thinking squares with reality: the full stature of our possibilities is the end.

Man wants fully to be, and intellect, something specific and integral to him, wants fully to be. It wants to reach the full stature of its possibility. Wanting to know, as well as wanting to be, is a kind of insatiable hunger in us. Being

* John Dewey, *Reconstruction in Philosophy,* p. 186; the same idea reappears in Dewey's *Human Nature and Conduct* and his *Liberalism and Social Action.*

and knowing, and in a real sense only half-being and half-knowing—that is, so far, the story of man and of his anguish. Yet the intellect has many chances to develop thrown in its way. Events, suffering and experience challenge it to come into its own. Normally, it gets some of its best opportunities in the schools. Hence the school, whether at home, at church, at play or "at school," is a common-sense institution, and although established by man, it is at least a kind of "natural." As Dewey insisted, the mind wants to grow and the school gives it the best common chance to grow.

The school is a place and time of leisure for intellectual growth. That is what it usually has been, and in any society we need something to be just that. Thus a defence of the school as a fact and as an historical institution would be next door to a defence of nature or the world. I neither accept nor reject the world—there it is, and it does not occur to me to accept or reject it. The family is like that, a "natural," and so is the political body, and again the church or worship group. Each of these three is a "natural." A particular family or political body or church can worsen or be bettered, but all the time the institution, which can thus have its ups and downs, is there in some good or bad condition and is ineradicable. The school should be at least relatively like that, too, if we take "school" in the sense of the quasi-official time and place for intellectual growth.

It is hard for Americans, dominated by the pioneering and practical spirit, to allow such freedom simply for intellectual development. We are likely always to remain the most practical people. We want results; money talks; time is money; business is business; pigs is pigs. We want to get on and do things. We have been timed to cutting down forests, making land, building railroads and factories, fighting wars, feeding the world, and it is not surprising that

Dewey, our chief spokesman in education, should have pragmatized the schools to death.

Accordingly, the school as a time and place of leisure for seeing God and nature and man and in that sense a time and place for liberal and natural intellectual growth seems to the majority of American people a little nonsensical, and also to the crowds flocking today to college. The word "school" itself is originally from the Greek word meaning "leisure," and this, so far from meaning either action or a sort of dissipated idleness, has historically meant a time and place for liberal and contemplative life.

Now for the relevance of these ideas to the heart of the present book. In the first place, this writer says that, no matter how contrary to American customs and presuppositions, it would be good for Protestant and Catholic and Jewish schools on every level to exist, not primarily to save or spread the faith or to save morals and to "make people good," but to seek intellectual growth. Not primarily, we say, to keep the Jewish child a faithful Jew and the Christian child a faithful Christian, but to answer the demands of nature to know. Here our thought is in agreement with the tradition of Western learning, though to declare for free intellectual ends may be asking a good deal of the American Protestant and Catholic and synagogue schools. Church-related schools were set up for something else and are being set up for something else. They do seek intellectual ends, but they seek them as an after-thought and as playing second fiddle to saving the faith of the Jew and the Christian. Perhaps even for their own purposes, they miss the point. Perhaps they would better serve even their non-intellectual ends if they were engaged with a more single-minded passion in the pursuit of intellectual ends.

It is true that on the intellectual basis suggested by us, church-related schools among Jews and Christians would

never have been at all in the first place. Harvard, for
example, was established to save a faith and make it look
good. But what we are asking is whether it is not possibly
time for Catholic and Protestant and Jewish schools in
America to begin to take the good of intellect as their
direct and proper good, and, at least on the higher levels
of college and university, as their consuming good.

We have always liked the vigorous remarks made in the
1920's by the late Jesuit, George Bull, regarding this question. He said that the Catholic educator's enemies often
turn out to be people of his own household, and we suppose the same might hold for the Jewish or Protestant
educator. "They [of the household] call upon the ultimate
objective of all Catholic life, the glory of God and the
salvation of souls, and attempt to make this do duty as
the immediate and specific object of education. They have
forgotten that the end of education, as such, is specific
and distinct from the end of missionary activity; that to
confound the ultimate end of both with the formal and
immediate object of each, is to introduce disorder into the
whole Catholic scheme."

In sum, we hold that schools of any religion or no religion
at all and on any level might operate primarily and directly
for learning as learning—and not as apologetics and propaganda for church or state or Communism or capitalism
or the military; not to convert or to save souls, not to save
the faith or morals of students, not to make people good,
and not to help individuals make money. This would apply
to Christian or Jewish schools, or schools of any or no reli-
ion. Schools do seek learning as learning. That is obvious.
But they often fail to do so, and we are aware that our
position must be shocking for practical-minded souls.

Why then should we have Catholic and Protestant and
Jewish schools? Do not the public schools, tax-supported,

do this job? These questions bring us back to the main positive point of the present chapter. Let us say that we need such schools not simply for knowledge, but for "adequacy of knowledge." We accept this summary, "adequacy of knowledge," as made by Dietrich von Hildebrand in his "Conception of a Catholic University" (in Kotschnig's *The University in a Changing World*).* The statement is laconic and even cryptic, and could only be a scandal to university people who, living so long in a secularist climate, had come to take their answers as final; today, as we remarked, they are far less confident. Knowledge or intellectual growth is the object of the Jewish or Christian school, as it is of any school. But the special object of these schools may be summed up as "adequacy of knowledge." Let us try to bring out the meaning of this phrase.

The centuries-old notion, which we take to be permanently valid and important, is that there is an overflow from faith into some areas of knowledge. Above all, there would be an overflow into what we know about man and God and their inter-relations, and thus into philosophy, sometimes into social science and ethics and into the content of literature and the arts. The overflow would not necessarily be into every cranny of all these areas, but in fact and inevitably into them. The classic summaries of the notion are two well-known formulas: *Fides quaerens intellectum,* and *Credo ut intelligam.* Take the first formula, "faith seeking to understand." The three following sentences explain what it means. If people believe such and such things about man and God and their inter-relations, somebody is going sooner or later to try to prove some of those things which, up to his time, had been taken on the ground

* The work is unavailable, but von Hildebrand's chapter, slightly revised, re-appeared as "Catholicism and unprejudiced knowledge" in his *The New Tower of Babel.* New York: Kenedy, 1953.

of belief-knowledge. If he does prove them, he and others will henceforth have them, not simply on the ground of belief-knowledge, but on the ground of scientific knowledge. Believers thereby have available a more adequate knowledge than have non-believers.

The work in thirteenth century universities is the prime example of this effort of faith to get a philosophical understanding of itself. But it is an effort always being made by Jews and Christians. Spinoza is an interesting test case. He says that his philosophy is not influenced by the Bible and by his strict Jewish training. But a second glance at his work will show the contrary. His choice of subjects in his work on Theology and Politics is obviously influenced by the Bible, and the very first sentence of his most famous work, his *Ethics*, contains the phrase "whose essence involves existence." This phrase is from a basic thesis in Jewish and Christian philosophy, a thesis which to begin with was accepted on the word of God to Moses. "Faith seeking to understand" means that some great scholars such as Spinoza sometimes try to get a naturally based knowledge of some truths formerly grasped only on another basis.

In this regard, faith helps in two ways toward knowledge. First, it keeps the believer, if he is of an inquiring turn, asking questions: when we say that experience asks questions, the experience of faith or believing is not excluded. For example, the idea of "person," never greatly or formally developed by Western pagan philosophers, is found by experience to be central in Christianity, and this central position of the person has prompted and in fact forced philosophers to develop a philosophy of "person." Once this development got under way and once the person was seen as at the apex of all things, the whole of social philosophy had to be reconsidered and newly and more justly developed. Take the almost offhand formula of Aquinas: "Man is not subordinate in all that he is and all that he has to any political community." This truth, so basic to democratic theory and life, was not grasped by either Plato or Aristotle, great as these thinkers were; and in *Paideia*, his consummate work on Greek moral ideals, Werner Jaeger, himself certainly not a man partial to Christian or democratic interpretations, shows that the Greeks even at their height kept falling back into subordinating man wholly to the state. Secondly, faith keeps suggesting answers. It says things significant for philosophy and sociology and culture as well as for theology. It says, for example, that man's evil-doing is a sin as surely as it says that God is pure being.

The second formula, *Credo ut intelligam*, as it works out is even more striking. To be on the safe side, we may under-translate it with a series of qualifiers. Then it reads: I believe, and, believing, perhaps I will be better able to understand some things. With the help and lead of believed truths, perhaps some Jews and Christians will be better able than other men to understand something or other.

If they ever did better understand anything or if they ever will, then Judeo-Christian learning, backed above all by the Bible, is thereby born, and at that point is able to add a new dimension to learning.* Hence the idea of "adequacy." If such an understanding accrues, some secularists also, so far as affected by a Judeo-Christian climate, may more or less inadvertently slough some of their secularist hide and (we think) achieve, so far, something at

---

* On this new dimension, see, e.g., Samuel Stumpf, "Theology and Jurisprudence" in *The Christian Scholar*, 40 (1957), 169-193: "it is precisely because it seeks to broaden the context within which law is to be studied that theology is so urgently concerned with jurisprudence . . ."

least akin to Judeo-Christian learning. As Mortimer Adler has suggested, if Thomas Aquinas, led by Revelation, is able to comprehend in philosophy some things otherwise extremely difficult of access, perhaps he will be able to teach those things to others who are not led by Revelation.

This new dimension and the big difference mentioned earlier are one and the same. Take a few instances. Believing in the word of God and the word and life of Christ, believers have—St. Paul actually had—a better chance to understand the unity of all men, the oneness of the world, the dignity of man, the sacredness and quasi-divine quality in every man. Not that secularists have to miss these truths, or that the ruck and run of believers will surely grasp and apply them. It is a long way from lip service to an undiluted understanding of man and an uncompromised and lived love of man in matters interracial, international, interfaith. The pagan Aristotle made two great points here. One is that repeating lines like an actor on the stage makes no man good. The other is that a man (or a group), living for a long time in an evil way as regards some basic matters, comes to lose sight of first principles: we know that an alcoholic does, and we have reason to conclude that a man or a group living on the assumption of interracial superiority does lose sight of basic principles.

We are not saved either for understanding or for right living by repeating the lines of our Christian, Jewish or secularist faiths. Without a certain type of works, faith is dead, and the theoretic and practical learning that might accrue from truths believed is never born. Our position, nevertheless, stands up. It is that believers in the word of God, if they are really believers and doers of the word, have a better chance to sense certain natural, unrevealed truths and perhaps ultimately to begin to understand them. That is what Immanuel Kant was saying when he said that, for all his depth studies in philosophy, the average saintly old woman understood moral philosophy better than he did.

Believing, perhaps men will come to understand. With an iron curtain of unbelief, it is going to be much more difficult. Think again about the unity of man and the dignity of man. Each of these is difficult and is extremely important. Where Aristotle speaks of losing sight of first principles (*Ethics*, VI, c.5), Sir David Ross translates the lines to read: The bad man "forthwith fails to see" the principles. They should be translated: The bad man does not at once see the principles; as a result he does not keep them constantly on tap. And the following are principles that man needs to keep constantly on tap—

> That man is to love man.
> That all men are one.
> That any man in his life and intelligence and
>   freedom has a sacred dignity and quasi-
>   divine quality.
> That man is to love God.
> That man is to fear God and to fear sin.

And so on for scores of practical and of theoretic truths, many of them of immense importance to the social order. All these are naturally knowable, and various pagans, such as Aristotle and Plato and Seneca, have known some of them. We hold that the man believing those truths on the word of God has a better chance to understand at least some of them than the man not believing them on the word of God. If the truths are believed and lived, they tend to filter through to the whole mass of common people. And truths such as those mentioned—e.g., that in regard to mankind's unity and that in regard to every man's hands-off dignity—are truths that men live by.

For twenty years the philosopher Jacques Maritain wrestled with phases of this question before he finally formulated what he designates as "Christian philosophy." Maritain explains his position by noting that although a man is a man whether slave or free, the condition makes a difference. Philosophy likewise is philosophy whether the man philosophizing is in a Christian or a pagan condition, but on many points the condition is sure to make a difference.* Also, says Maritain, a comparable difference is to be expected, proper allowances being made, for understandings achievable by the historian, the poet, and the exegete.

Grant that a misled believer can turn rabid and become a hypocrite, a grand inquisitor and a dictator. Even so, our declarations on the believer and the iron curtain of unbelief stand. What is more important, they hold for the tone and direction of a whole society's believing and knowing as well as for the individual's. The belief that God has become man is sure to make a difference to a society's and an era's understanding of God and man. So too for the belief that God is a person, and the belief that God is our father. It makes a difference or it does not—that is the whole point which may be summarily formulated as follows. The human race believing theoretic truths X, Y, Z and practical truths A, B, C on God's word is more likely to come to a natural understanding of those truths than the human race not believing those truths on God's word.

According to the view being expressed, a Jewish or a Christian scholar would be a man whose learning has been enriched by some of those theoretic or practical truths, a man who knows some truths outright or some truths

* Jacques Maritain, *An Essay on Christian Philosophy*. Tr. by Edward Flannery. New York: Philosophical Library, 1955.

better because he has believed. It does not matter what the man's field of learning, at least within the humanities. He knows truths or he better knows truths because he has first believed. That is our position and we will not let any secularist a priori or any propaganda-and-apologetic a priori scare us away from it. St. Augustine put it in the double negative in words from Isaias (vii, 9): "Unless you had first believed, you would not have understood." Those words no doubt are shocking, if our primary concern is not knowledge and not the "adequacy" attainable in Judeo-Christian knowledge, but looking good to secularist theory. Let us, however, be moderate and tone Augustine's words down to read: Believing, perhaps you will have a better chance to understand some things.

The truth contained in Augustine's words is evident in many ordinary instances. If a child could come to school, at home or at school, as an absolute sceptic, he could not learn anything. Believing, he has a chance even in difficult matters. If I first believe that Einstein possibly has something, I will have a better chance to understand. And if I finally do understand, my belief, based on the man's word, has not hurt my understanding. On the contrary, it has helped. It is odd that so many shy away in theory from so obvious a fact. From infancy there is in all men this constant tendency to translate truths believed on man's or God's word into truths understood. It is a good and absolutely necessary habit. Without it the race would remain in its infancy.

In this case we can readily see that belief on man's word as well as on God's word precedes and influences much of anyone's learning. A philosophy of education can only be naive if it omits this common basic fact regarding how children learn. The psychology of it is well expressed by each of two authors, one medieval, the other contemporary.

In his treatise on Truth (q.14, a.10) Aquinas remarks that a person, at first imperfect in knowledge, needs the help of an instructor if he is to proceed to perfection of knowledge in any particular field. The instructor himself needs to have grasped the bases of the knowledge in question. But the beginner does not at once comprehend the bases of the more subtle truths involved in it. That is why the good teacher "hands to him" matters the grounds and bases of which the student will later know, once he has sufficiently developed a habit in the given science. Aquinas concludes: "And so it is said that the learner has to believe. Otherwise he cannot reach perfect knowledge. I mean unless he accepts things given to him at the outset."

The same observations hold for sciences, e.g., physics and mathematics. The first step in science—and here we must disagree with Dewey—is not problem-solving or a felt need, but an act of faith and belief. So at any rate says our second author. Michael Polyani in a remarkable passage shows how the beginner learns in science.* The future scientist, says Dr. Polyani, is attracted by popular literature or by schoolwork in science before he can form any idea of scientific work. The morsels of science he picks up whet his appetite and hint at worlds yet unknown. As a result the youth begins to guess at a vast system of valid thought and endless discovery, and if he has good luck he meets a teacher whose work he admires and who leads him on to methods of investigation. Polyani continues:

> At every stage of his progress towards this end he is urged on by the belief that certain things as yet beyond his knowledge and even understanding are on the whole true and valuable . . . This represents a recognition of

* Michael Polyani. *Science, Faith and Society*. London, Oxford Press, 1946; pp. 30-31.

the authority of that which he is going to learn and of those from whom he is going to learn it. It is the same attitude as that of the child listening to its mother's voice and absorbing the meaning of speech. Both are based on an implicit belief in the significance and truth of the context which the learner is trying to master. A child could never learn to speak if it assumed that the words which are used in its hearing are meaningless; or even if it assumed that five words out of ten so used are meaningless. And similarly no one can become a scientist unless he presumes that the scientific doctrine and method are fundamentally sound and that their ultimate premisses can be unquestionably accepted. We have here an instance of the process described epigrammatically by the Christian Church Fathers in the words: *fides quaerens intellectum*, faith in search of understanding.

Even in learning to speak, the child learns by first believing that the words and ideas ringing in his ears make sense. Just so, the budding scientist learns by first believing, and his first believing that Einstein has something to teach is a help to his finally coming to know. Now our position, as is evident, is at one with that of Aquinas and Polyani, since our claim is that believing on God's word—and this belief is itself a belief-knowledge, or at least a belief not devoid of knowledge—can well be a first step leading to the knowledge of many things.

Two minor points must be disposed of. First, the truths we speak of are positive truths. Of course, faith on man's or God's word teaches that some things are not true, and then for better or worse, the believer assumes that there is no use trying to prove those things. That is what is meant by saying that faith, either human or divine, is a "negative norm." Far more important for the total efflorescence of learning is the body of truths which, once believed, is more likely to become known, and, if already known, to become better known because it is first believed on man's or God's word. We mean the "total efflorescence of learning" in a particular mind, and also in a community of students and scholars, and in the whole Western and Eastern world. To cite again some truths translated from divine faith to knowledge, let us mention truths about man's goodness, the goodness of all nature, the natural unity of mankind, a balance between hope and fear, between knowing man's greatness and his littleness—hence a sane optimism—truths about God's being, and about the dignity and sacredness of human life, even in the aged, the infirm and unborn. Negative truths, yes, matters that are known to be untrue; and positive truths, matters which we come to know to be true. The Judeo-Christian world is the beneficiary of both types.

The second point to be disposed of is a strange and unhappy alliance. As we said, the old notion is that Catholic schools, and no doubt Jewish or Protestant schools, are to be directly concerned with apologetics and defending the faith. This old notion (mistaken—we claim—in the first place) has made a freak alliance with secularism in the case of many American Catholic scholarly men, and perhaps of some Protestants and Jews, too. A "Christian scholar" is assumed by these Catholic men of good will to be a Christian who is a scholar. It seems as simple as that. But what it really comes to is a cross between fideism and secularism. In his learning, the scholar secularizes strongly, and in his daily life believes even more strongly. Then he is thought to be automatically a Christian scholar. The scholar denudes his learning of anything that has the least positive relationship to faith, and in his learning he is as secularist as the next fellow. But he believes, all the same. Then he regards himself as a model Christian scholar. Faith here, and learning there, each of them kept in an airtight compartment. For this view, Descartes, who was at once a Christian and a scholar, would be the ideal man. On this view, Descartes would be a Christian scholar and his learning would be Christian—because, a savant and learned in mathematics and philosophy, he was also a Christian; and a group of a dozen or more Descartes working together would automatically form the grandest Christian college or university.

We strongly disagree and cannot by any means accept such a view. Amass all the Descartes of the last three centuries—and there are a lot of them—and the result would indeed be learning, but it would be on the basis of a secularist fideism, and would not be a Christian learning. Its bearers could not form a Christian university. What we really get as a Catholic or Protestant or Jewish university is a confusion, a mixed-up thing, a hybrid between a Judeo-Christian university and a secularist one. Nevertheless, one reason suggested by some Christians of good will why we should favor this secularist fideism is that otherwise we would greatly scandalize secularist non-fideists. Our reply is twofold. We do not want either fideists or secularists or a cross between them. Secondly, if there is any such thing as a possible or actual Judeo-Christian learning —say, in social science, philosophy and the content of literature and the arts—then by all means let us investigate and develop this learning, let scandal unfortunately fall where it will.

At least in America the common thing is that, although the fideistic secularist may be a scholar, he is up to his ears in apologetics. What the fideistic secularist wants is that the sheer secularist will be able to say: "Look at these fine fideistic secularists—they are Christians and, believe it or not, they are scholars. They are scholars in spite of the fact that they are Christians. They are Christians, but you would have to go to the department of fideism to find it out."

Our view is positive. It is that a Judeo-Christian learning has existed, that it now exists, and that ideally it is, like any learning, alive and growing and coming more and more into existence. Of its nature, it has a dynamism and "go" to it.

If such a learning in any way exists, it is important for the education of Americans, and even for their understanding of themselves, and also in view of the world situation. Besides, we hold that this Judeo-Christian learning could justify Jewish and Christian schools. We doubt that anything else, such as apologetics and propaganda or "making people good," does justify them as schools, above all on the higher levels, and we doubt that in the long run anything else could justify them. For wherever we try denaturing things, we may at best expect unfortunate results.

We doubt that in the continuing world crisis, a mere secularism in learning or life can do much for mankind. For we must repeat that mere secularism is only one remove from Communist revolutionary secularism.

The ideal is not two truths shut off from each other, a fideistic truth and a sheer secularist positivist truth; but one Judeo-Christian truth. St. Jerome said that the Christian may well assimilate as a part of his one integral truth the truths achieved by pagans; to do this requires work, of course, as all vital, creative learning requires work. At just Jerome's time, St. Augustine took the same position and expressed it in an unforgettable figure. He said that as the Jews, in order to store their sacred articles, were justified in appropriating vessels belonging to the Egyptians, so the Christians may appropriate any valid learning of the pagans. Augustine claimed that "pagan learning" belongs more rightly to Christians than to its pagan discoverers. Our own position is that truth belongs to mankind, and Christians may pillage the learning of Plato and Euclid and of anyone else. Christians may have all that learning, and then some—that is the point of Jerome and Augustine, and it is our positive point.

Our conclusion is simple. We say that to be unwilling at least to have the question raised whether there possibly is a Judeo-Christian learning would be unworthy of any scholar. And, given the remarkable Judeo-Christian background of Western learning, not to be raising the question would be unworthy of any "Jewish university," any "Christian university," any fideist-secularist university and any secularist university.

CHAPTER 6

A Plan of Action

Education falls within the range of freedom and for that reason many and various good things can be done to help toward educating in literacy of any type. In educational practices we are always seeking an end which is multiple and variegated, and the means to it may be arranged in any of several effective ways. Here of course we speak for religious literacy, in part through schools. Some conditions must be met, however, and are presupposed if we are to have religious literacy in and through American public schools, to reintroduce God in any notable way into the public-school experience of children, and also if we are to do a good job of letting God speak in church-related schools. Personally, our minimum hope for improvement is that we shall begin to allow at least high-school students in public schools to learn something of religion as a social phenomenon. This is not a big lot to ask and we should not have to bombard Mars to get it.

Among conditions, a simple one is that to reach such ends we must acquire a realistic and honest approach to

American history and the Constitution, and also to world history and above all to recent anthropological studies by such men as Bidney, Evans-Pritchard, the self-revised Kluckhohn, and the late Ralph Linton. Not only Sir James Frazer but Sumner is dead. One might contend that Sumner had blindly empiricized and that therefore his work was stillborn; Sir James at least wrote imaginatively and glamorously. Some of the most confident positions in Ruth Benedict's charming productions are out of date and have to be scrapped. What is needed in this regard is a mature mind on the subject of religion as something given in mankind's total experience and of course as something sticking out in our American experience, and something seemingly demanded in man's struggles. A more mature mind should progressively mean both more respect for man and a more democratic view of human reality.

That first condition is compound and will not be taken care of in a day. A second condition is that religious teachers and preachers be widely and deeply, as well as professionally, educated. We have a right not to be suffering from their narrowness. As already indicated, that is much to ask, given the historical background and the present state of seminary studies in America. A mere *ad hoc* education shuts the religionist and his religion up in a corner. That is no proper place for any man in modern times. In fact, the religionist himself, to do his work well for persons and society, needs everything. He needs a "liberal liberal" education and, no doubt as part of that, a real as well as an appreciative awareness of religion as a global phenomenon and as both a builder and a maintainer of civilizations.

To be honest and realistic at all, church-related educators as well as others must be open-minded enough to see that all segments of American society today depend on the public schools and that what happens to the public schools happens to America. Putting the matter in the lowest key, we must say that we need those schools because for the vast majority no other schools are available or are likely to become available. Catholics perhaps have more parochial grade and high schools than have all other religions combined. Yet the formal book-learning of Catholics in America is going to remain largely in and through public schools. About half the Catholic grade-schoolers and a bigger percentage of all Catholic high-schoolers are in public schools. For that reason, Catholics in America are obligated to support and promote excellence in public schooling. But that is not the only or the main reason. Even if any group such as Quakers or Mennonites or Catholics were to have all its children in its own private schools, the members of that group would still be morally bound as citizens to work with all men of good will to help make our public schools as good as possible. In passing we say that it is a sign of health in American educational life that a vigorous debate is going on relative to the quality of school work, especially on the high-school level. For our part we are delighted to see the sides squared off against each other; e.g., Bestor and Rickover versus Trump and Conant.*

For its very life the nation needs the best producible public schools. At the same time, our early American experience has shown that public schools are not a pre-

---

* In his *Educational Wastelands* and *The Restoration of Education*, Arthur Bestor has been a pioneer. Rear Admiral H. G. Rickover's *Education and Freedom* (New York: Dutton, 1959) has at least tried to make the nation wake up. J. Lloyd Trump's *Images of the Future* (2400 Gregory Hall, Urbana, Ill., 1959) is, like James B. Conant's *The American Public High School Today* (New York: Doubleday, 1959), more hopeful that the public high school can, with a moderate amount of readjustment, come up to its proper potential.

requisite for democracy. As Christian Gauss said *: "Recent attempts to find in the exclusion of all forms of instruction in religion a fundamental element in the American tradition of higher education have therefore no warrant in our earlier educational history." The experience of other democratic nations such as England and Ireland has for generations shown the same thing. Winston Churchill went to a private school, and one need not be an Anglophile to say that Churchill always stood as a democratic force for and with his people. Of course, Americans are, in important ways, in a different case. With us, public schools have for over a century been a potent melting pot and a kind of democratic mill. They continue and must continue to be that. Just think of the Puerto Ricans pouring into New York City and Detroit and of the colored people pouring into Northern cities (thirty-five thousand a year into Chicago). We have to keep making one world out of many worlds: *e pluribus unum.* Helping with that task through schools and otherwise is the duty of all who believe in America. For these reasons those parents who choose to patronize private schools for religious or scientific values or for freedom must make sure that their children find ways, at home and at school, of compensating for the possible loss of democratic-making opportunities. At the same time we cannot for a moment bless anyone who takes it on himself to harass in any way the life and freedoms of private schools.

If all of us must work to make all schools excellent, we must concede that a really tough part of that general assignment is how to teach religion in public schools. The old hush-up method, dominant since the time of Horace

* Christian Gauss on page 8 of a work edited by him: *The Teaching of Religion in American Higher Education.* New York: Ronald, 1951.

Mann, will solve few important problems. As we have seen, the "religion in education" problem is twofold: how to teach religion in public schools without violating the right of religious liberty, and, secondly, how to teach it or have it taught in all types of schools without in any instance giving official breaks to any particular church. Congress shall make no law "concerning" or "preventing." Today, surely, "preventing" the free exercise of teaching is a more likely danger than setting up an established church, or aiding and abetting any church.

The problem as we noted is not so unthinkable as it was forty and fifty and a hundred years ago. For several reasons that add up, both the "how" and the fact of religion's return to public schools show promise. This is above all true of the colleges and universities, whence we may hope it will in time trickle down to lower schools. Why the promise? First, because more people see the need of religion in view of international crises and in view of the domestic moral crisis in children and adults. Secondly, because the highest court in America, unlike any possible court in the totalitarian world, is officially allowing the state to "adjust its schedule" of events in schools to the traditions and demands of the people; i.e., the court is taking account of democracy and American history. Thirdly, because teachers therefore are (we hope) going eventually to be less scared to take up the problem of studying and teaching religion. Fourthly, because in several state universities such as Iowa and Michigan State, theology, often called "religion," is being taught on the undergraduate level by Jews and Catholics and Protestants; in some "non-sectarian" universities such as Princeton and Yale, Protestant theology is taught, and at least Harvard is determined to round out its theological offerings with a chair of Roman Catholic studies. Lastly, because some of the best Protestant leadership is beginning to show itself free and uninhibited and traditional in its view of the place of religious studies in public schools on all levels.

On the problem of religion's return to the college and university, both state and non-sectarian, Merrimon Cuninggim's study * is exceedingly instructive and encouraging. He records that in state institutions administrators had for a time felt that "their hands were tied" but now they experience "more freedom," and his thesis is that "secularization is past and that administrative responsibility for religion is increasingly being recognized." Many colleges and universities, he says, have significant programs for teaching religion, among them Yale, Princeton, Duke, Northwestern, Chicago, Denison. He says that "leaders among tax-supported institutions concerned about religion" include these universities: Iowa, Pennsylvania State, Florida, Connecticut, and Michigan. As of 1947, he found that 21 out of 70 state institutions or 30 per cent had a department of religion in the regular curriculum.

Particular things which can be done in this progressively favorable climate will be suggested in the following pages. The suggested matters are approaches which are being explored or will have to be explored.

One big point, never completely missed by anyone competent to teach in any type of school, is teaching religion within the context of other subjects. In this regard, there is no necessary preaching or indoctrinating. Just one thing is necessary, and that is teaching. Theology is intrinsically related to each of many non-theological studies. This means that we cannot teach any subject at least in the humanities without raising and answering theological questions. Try to teach Shakespeare purged of reference to theology.

* Cuninggim, *The College Seeks Religion,* Yale University Press, 1947; pp. 2, 3, 183-218, 298-301.

Try to teach "Alice in Wonderland" and leave out all hint of theology. What would "Christopher Robin is saying his prayers" mean once we tried to delete what it does mean? Even if we translated it, "Secularist Joe is defying your gods," we would raise theological questions. "Getting and spending we lay waste our powers . . . Great God, I'd rather be a pagan suckled in a creed outworn." If we try to teach Wordsworth's or anyone's poetry, we are faced with theological issues, and of course the poets include many besides Dante and Milton. If a fourth-grade class studies the American Indians, some child is sure to ask about the Indians' religion and ways of worship, and the whole class is of course exposed—alas for an absolute separation "wall"—to the fact of Christian missionaries among the Indians. The question at bottom is whether we are free to teach the truth and whether we are honest or dishonest.

In Western history, the teacher inevitably encounters the same problem. Christmas without Christ and the Mass would be unreal and dishonest educational diet, and Thanksgiving without God and theologies would be nonsense: and whatever our own religion, we have no right as educators to be dishonest or nonsensical. We could not honestly teach Washington's Farewell, Lincoln's Second Inaugural, the Gettyburg Address, or Truman's first broadcast as president, or the Presidents' relation to the history of Thanksgiving, if we insisted that the religious acts and professions of famous Americans, and their theological presuppositions, must have no place in public or other schools. "Our Fathers' God, to Thee, Author of liberty . . . Long may our land be bright with freedom's holy light. Protect us by Thy might, Great God, our King!"

Words must be allowed to mean just what they mean. We may not tolerate dishonest teaching in any school.

We may not, under cover of the "separation" principle, or under cover of any group's feelings or advantage, try hedging and pretending that the events of history never happened. We may not invent a "wall" to hide the truth.

History, literature, art and philosophy would have to go if theology had to go. All history would be eviscerated and misrepresented, world history, Western history, as influenced especially by Jews and Christians and Mohammedans, and American history.

In relation to American history this point of "involvement" has been best stated by two Americans. First, by Joseph F. Costanzo who says * in part:

> The fact of the involvement of religion in public education and the equally important fact that our American institutions presuppose a Supreme Being must be positively considered in . . . public schools for the transmission of the American heritage. Pedagogically, there is no special, peculiar difficulty preventing a teacher, no matter what his faith or lack of it, from teaching correctly to students, no matter what their faith or lack of it, the meaning of words and expressions, of facts and factors of American national history, which are theological, and . . . which are surely not without meaning to the Jewish, Protestant, and Catholic believers. We are not asking that teachers teach sectarian religion, nor even 'about religion' but that they simply explain what needs to be explained doctrinally in the course of teaching secular subjects. This can be done *correctly* no matter what the belief or lack of it in the teacher or the hearer . . . There is no violation of anybody's conscience.

Secondly, this point of the involvement of religion in all education was made with brevity and force by Justice

* Joseph F. Costanzo, S.J., "Religion in Public School Education." *Thought*, v. 31 (Summer, 1956), p. 18.

Jackson concurring in the McCollum decision, and we are happy to repeat his words in the present context. He said that although teaching a creed or catechism or ceremonial was out of the question, how is it possible "to isolate and cast out of secular education" all religious education? Perhaps, he said, it can be done in mathematics and some physical sciences, but not in the arts: not in music, painting, or architecture and certainly not in history. He continued: "The fact is that, for good or for ill, nearly everything in our culture worth transmitting, everything that gives meaning to life, is saturated with religious influences, derived from paganism, Judaism, Christianity—both Catholic and Protestant—and other faiths accepted by a large part of the world's people. One can hardly respect a system of education that would leave the student wholly ignorant of the currents of religious thought that move the world society for a part in which he is being prepared."

The involvement of religion in all education is so obvious that only a Communist would reject it, and at the cost of falsification, indoctrination and dishonesty. What we have said of the old "humanities" holds also for sociology, politics, economics, and anthropology. The question is whether we are scientific and honest enough to teach them. These subjects cannot be understood if denuded of reference to religion and theology, because they do not exist as so denuded. As Maritain * has said:

Theological problems and controversies have permeated the whole development of Western culture and civilization, and are still at work in its depths, in such a way that the one who would ignore them would be

* Jacques Maritain, *Education at the Crossroads.* Yale University Press, 1943; pp. 73-74.

fundamentally unable to grasp his own time and the meaning of its internal conflicts. Thus impaired, he would be like a barbarous and disarmed child walking amidst the queer and incomprehensible trees, fountains, statues, gardens, ruins, and buildings still under construction, of the old park of civilization.

Maritain goes on to say that such a one would miss everything. He would miss the intellectual and political history of modern times, the Reformation and Counter Reformation, the Pilgrim Fathers, the Rights of Man, Dante, Cervantes, Rabelais, Oscar Wilde and D. H. Lawrence, Madison and Jefferson, Goethe, Dostoevski and "even Karl Marx."

A man so schooled, and many of us are being more or less so schooled, would be cheated out of the chance to understand. He would fail to get a liberal education or any education at all.

Christian Gauss remarked on the urgency of the total problem, even on the lower levels. He said that we are encountering a condition of any decent education at all * : "Teachers of the arts and literature recognize that the over-secularization of our high-school education has left a blind spot on the mind of the average college freshman. This is equally true whether his parents are atheists, agnostics, or still allied to some religious denomination. The competent teacher, whatever his particular faith or lack of faith, finds that without an intelligent grounding in religious concepts, students cannot begin to understand subjects like Gothic architecture or Italian painting, Dante's *Divine Comedy*, Milton's *Paradise Lost* or Pascal's *Pensées*."

In short, this is an absolute. We must study religion at

* Christian Gauss, *op. cit.*, p. 18.

least when and where and as it is involved in the context. Otherwise, we have to remain uneducated.

For some years, a second suggestion found favor. People said the answer was to teach a "common core" of theological doctrine. And we must admit that this idea, just as idea, is excellent. Look at the basic doctrines on which Jews, Catholics and Protestants agree: one God exists, creator and father of all; God is a person; God can speak to man and has done so; love of God and man is the great commandment in the Law. To teach such matters as a common core would not be the same as to teach them as inevitably involved in history, sociology, art and literature, but as a sort of course in religion and theology. To teach those and related matters would be like giving a course in "Western religion."

Something or other that amounts to a "common core" is basic and essential, at least in college and if particular theologies are not in some way covered; otherwise the student is as completely lost as a child from Mars. But the "common core" idea has never worked out, on any level. Though it looks easy and is easy to name those central doctrines, even little children at home and at school could raise difficult questions: What is God? Why do we not see God? How do we know God? Is Christ God? On such questions the great Western groups themselves do not see eye to eye, so that a teacher possessed of the best intentions might end up by offending people. To be of use the method would require more maturity than our teachers and especially our children and their parents now possess. Besides, it might remain difficult to present any such "core" without affronting secularists and cutting across the "separation" principle objectively considered.

A third suggestion is far better, and, teaming with the teaching of religious matters where they occur in context, simply must be tried. Let us call it "What Believers Believe." This would not be a common core at all. It would be a set of particular cores, and is what is now called a study "about" religion. It thus should be able to avoid, not only ideally but really, the danger of indoctrination. It would be the factual study of religion in America and elsewhere, the study of what religion has historically been, and what it now is, and its influence, now or at any time, on culture and civilization. In short, this would be an objective study of religion, and indeed of religions and theologies.

Such a study would naturally break down into several parts: for example, what Jews believe; what Catholics believe; what Protestants believe. Under pressure of modern world-conditions, we might also consider ourselves invited to go farther, at least on the higher levels, and study what Mohammedans and Confucians believe, and, time permitting, what some or many primitives believe. Fortunately, for such comprehensive "courses" good books are available; it must suffice to mention Otto Karrer's *The Religions of Mankind.**

Schools might go a step farther, if feasible, and try to learn why this or that group believes what it believes. The matters believed and the reasons why are relevant and important for all believers and unbelievers, lay or clergy, but are especially relevant and important in the

* Otto Karrer, *The Religions of Mankind.* New York: Sheed and Ward, 1936. For lower levels, the one best comprehensive little book is Florence Mary Fitch, *One God: the Ways We Worship Him.* New York: Lothrop, Lee & Shepard, 1944. For particular religions, these are very good: Louis Finkelstein, *The Beliefs and Practices of Judaism.* New York: Devin-Adair, 1941; Josef Pieper and Heinz Raskop, *What Catholics Believe.* New York: Pantheon Books, 1951; and John Cogley, "What Is a Catholic?" (a pamphlet), Ave Maria Press, Notre Dame, Ind., 1953. On the higher levels, for the clash of religions in America see *Religion in America* edited by John Cogley. New York: Meridian, 1958.

education of religious leaders. This is so important and relevant that we would be for inviting the best available Jewish scholars and Protestant scholars into Catholic seminaries to enable future Catholic priests and bishops, and lay leaders, too, to know firsthand just what it is that Jews and Protestants believe, and just why. Of course we would want the favor reciprocated. We would want, for the good of the child and the nation, to have the best Catholic scholarship, in the persons of scholars, visiting our people at other seminaries, such as the Jewish Theological Seminary of America and Union Theological Seminary. What we seek at this point is that religious leaders should understand, honestly and objectively, the position of other believers. In all types of schools, it is understood that we may settle for nothing less than scientific, objective study, and for our part we are convinced that many American seminaries, whatever their religious affiliations, have historically been infected with rhetorical half-truths in regard to "competing religions." The author knows that Catholics sometimes "spout" without knowing whereof they speak. We may guess that the favor is returned. Indeed, we do not have to guess, for now and then reliable reports tell us that some Protestant ministers are irresponsible distortionists, not only in hillbilly areas, but in cities all over the nation.

The study which we are suggesting, of "What Believers Believe," belongs in all schools, public and private, technical and liberal, and is needed in the training of all citizens. Schools unwilling to accept the idea (implementing it would be another problem) should be held suspect. The study of "What Believers Believe" could be and should be an objective study of religious subject matter. It would be difficult, of course. That goes for the study of anything worth studying. Part of the difficulty would come from inveterate bad habits and attitudes, of misunderstanding and misrepresenting, of hostility toward people of other religions. * We may hope that this kind of unfair habit and attitude is on the way out.

Part of the difficulty would come from the fact that competent teachers of "What Believers Believe" would be rare and at first might be almost nonexistent, and certainly they would at first be far too few to man the public and private schools of America. These handicaps are obvious and are not altogether peculiar to the present subject matter. But we are an affluent nation believing in freedom and spending billions on education. Perhaps the problem is soluble, and especially today when the level of education is rising— in many suburbs it has reached a mid-college level—and when we are becoming more aware of the need for objectivity and excellence in education. Besides, we are a pioneering people, and in the present matter we must expect a need for vision, courage and sacrifice. In time we may, in seminaries and all types of schools, be able to approach the required maturity. After all, any nation has the problem of growing up.

The idea contained in "What Believers Believe" plainly has its merits. To begin with, the idea could be used and implemented to some extent on any level, and in technical high schools as well as in advanced creative work. No school is too public or too private for it. We need to presuppose only a modicum of intelligence and freedom. Not a high school in America can afford to try to do any longer without something of the kind. The present writer

---

* Writing in the *Saturday Review* (May 14, 1960), Samuel Hendel says of James A. Pike's and Richard Byfield's *A Roman Catholic in the White House* (New York: Doubleday, 1960), ". . . what emerges from the organization and emphases of the book as a whole is a highly biased presentation."

is a priest, and he must confess that his training both in public and private schools and the seminary, and his teaching in public and private schools and the seminary, have left him far too ignorant—let's say, simply ignorant—of what orthodox or unorthodox Jews believe and of what such important groups as Lutherans and Presbyterians in America believe.

Religious groups in most instances teach religion with great earnestness to their own constituencies. Then they stop at that. Then some day we are all surprised to find how ignorant and intolerant we are. Many Jewish children are well taught their religion at home and in the synagogue schools. But what a shame it is that they do not know well, appreciate and sympathize deeply with Christian beliefs, many of which so greatly honor the Jewish people. It is a shame that Catholic grade and high school children, assiduously taught their religion, do not know well both the rich and decisive Jewish background of it and the Protestant agreement with it and challenge to it. Protestants, too, like to be sealed up in Protestant cells. Would it not be wonderful for all concerned to have Catholic nuns competent to teach, at least in high schools, what Protestantism means in our times and what the Jewish religion has meant for many centuries? Think, too, what it would mean for the liberal education of our people and the good of the nation if Jews and Protestants, in and out of school, were able to convey to children an appreciative understanding of the mere fact that at least 90,000 Catholic nuns are teaching in American schools.

It is an odd and undemocratic thing to live in the same street with people and never know what they believe. Every man a foreigner to his neighbor. In our opinion, that is not right. Once upon a time, it was perhaps conceivably tolerable. But with modern travel and easy com-

munications, times have changed. The simple truth is that
we ought to know our neighbors better. And that is not
half the story. For on top of all that, we are at a new
stage in history in this matter of "neighbors." Willy-nilly,
we are next door to the whole world. We know that it is
against the grain for isolationists even to look at that fact.
But today we must begin to find out, all of us, what Ori-
entals believe, and why they believe as they believe. So
we had better begin this sort of learning in our own back-
yards.

Any liberally educated person therefore is going to have
to know what his neighbors think about God and man and
man's destiny, and much more any person qualified to
become a leader in society and to teach on any level. To
get a decent modicum of such learning may help us to
cross some bothersome bridges. Any of us, teachers or
others, really understanding the beliefs held and lived
by persons of other belief-groups would come to have an
increasing respect and love for those persons. So much
may be confidently predicted. To stand off as we now do
and not know at all the deepest faiths by which others
live cannot make for respect and love. Most of us are unfortunately lodged in that stand-off fix. There is even good
reason to guess that many priests, rabbis and preachers lack
a sympathetic and intimate knowledge of each other's
theologies.

To that democratic commandment, "Know thy neighbor's faith," we add another closely related one. Schools
must begin to know each other. In cities and many towns,
we have two school systems, private and public, at least
on the grade and secondary levels. These two must learn
how they can be much closer to each other. Their fences
are high now. "Private" and "public" keep looking across
an immense space and conjecturing and suspecting. Some-

times they have some bit of inter-school games, but seldom anything more.

The trouble is that they do not know and love or even so much as respect each other. How could they be expected to when they rarely if ever cross each other's doorstep? Now and then a blast comes from a big "public" school crowd, as that emanating from a group in session at Columbia University in 1959: contrary to American history, this group alleged that private schools are undemocratic. Then the other side squares off. A big churchman lets loose his heavy guns.

Our own position is that all of this is bad business, bad for patriotism, and truth, and charity, and education. Let us look at the schools together. Private schools are so indigenous to America and so much with us that teachers in a public school are ill-prepared and poor teachers if they do not know from the inside the work and life of American private schools. The same holds for teachers in private schools who should be bound by an oath of office to visit public schools and to hobnob with teachers and students in those schools. As an old public-school teacher has said, "Mixing melts a lot of ice." Knowing from the inside—that is what we insist on. No more long-range shots. An exchange of teachers between the two kinds would make good educational sense, and good horse sense.

In this vital matter of knowing or not knowing American schools from the inside, the vast majority of teachers in both types of schools today are negligent and are guilty of obscurantism.

I suppose it may be tolerable for soldiers or farmers or shoplifters not to know either type of school. But I am saying that teachers on each shift, public and private, are obliged to know both types. Failure to state a relevant psychological law is a notable defect in modern psychology.

This law is as follows. When groups such as capital and labor or Jew and non-Jew are geographically close to each other, and yet never consort so as to know and respect and love one another, an unnatural gap develops and, sure as fire, nature will fill it in with guesses, suspicions, and even with wildly aimed chunks of hate. The groups are meant by nature and God to know and love and respect each other. Nature hates a psychological vacuum and soon fills it up with trash. That is just what sometimes happens between the two school systems.

Charles Lamb is reputed to have said that he hated a certain man. Told that he did not even know the man, Lamb said: "Of course not. If we knew a man, we surely would not hate him." The schools must come to know each other. That is an ethical "must," and a religious, a political and an educational "must." If they come to know each other, they will have reason to respect each other, a thing that cannot be done on the basis of their present silly ignorance.

Would that mean a return to learning something about religion in American schools? We hope so! We are sure that it is at least a necessary condition for any such learning. An eye for an eye leaves us far off from religion.

Up to this point we have suggested four things that can be done, at least step by step and in various degrees, toward restoring some sense and balance in the matter of instruction in religion. These four are, first, that the religious and theological matters inevitably coming up in non-theological studies, from the kindergarten through college, are to be objectively considered just as are any other matters inevitably coming up. Secondly, the common core idea which in its nature is basic and a minimum, but probably can be managed only on higher levels, if at all. Thirdly, what believers believe.* Fourthly, some cross-fertilization between private and public schools on all levels.

Each of the four can be better handled where teachers and students are more mature and best handled in college and university where many students begin to be grown up and where professors in private and public institutions have more knowledge and freedom than on lower levels. Of course, professors can be immature even in universities: remember that many an American professor came in recently from a cornfield (which he never understood, either). If we are to trust Buckley's lively essay on God and man at Yale, men who are scholars in other areas can be unscientific and puerile on theological questions; reviewing Buckley in the *London Tablet*, Christopher Hollis, M.P., said that, granting the remarks quoted by Buckley to be accurate and representative, American criticism of religion is astonishingly crude. This crudity, immaturity and puerility on religion is one of our national problems in education, and is matched at times by the crudity and childishness of much of the rhetoric we are exposed to in the name of religious teaching and preaching.

Here we need two things which may be hard to obtain. In university professors, we need a spirit of reverence toward religion—let us say, at least reverence toward man and man's traditions, including his beliefs in God. In re-

* Those three matters are being well said by others: e.g., by W. C. Bower, "A Proposed Program for Achieving the Role of Religion in Education." *Religious Education*, v. 50 (July-Aug. 1955); F. Ernest Johnson, "Summary of Policies and Recommendations of the American Council on Education Committee on Religion and Education." *Religious Education*, v. 52 (July-Aug. 1957); F. Ernest Johnson, *American Education and Religion*. Harper, 1952; esp. chapters 1 and 12; Joseph F. Costanzo, "Religion in Public School Education." *Thought*, v. 31 (Summer, 1956); Ellis Ford Hartford, *Moral Values in Public Education*, Harper, 1958; and Neil Gerard McCluskey, *Public Schools and Moral Education*, Columbia University Press, 1958.

ligious leaders, we need (as noted above) a spirit of objectivity, respecting data from many sciences such as anthropology, biology, psychology and history.

This coming of age and achieving habits of scientific and mature judgment on human things will require time and patience and will never be perfectly and once for all accomplished. All the same, good things are being done, even in high schools.

To see what can readily be done, let us take an actual case of teaching religion, a course on what believers believe and how they worship.

A Michigan teacher has reported * that in working in a public school with tenth graders in a course designed to unify social studies and to improve human relations, she and the students had studied problems of race and the home and the classroom, but had shied away from religion. Even so, this course in "Living Together in Today's World" had meant to be honest and thorough and objective. Dodging religion came as usual from fear on the teacher's part, but not on the students' part. Then teacher and students plunged into these obvious question: Why is religion so important? How do our neighbors worship, and why do they worship in different ways? What effect has religion on our government? Has our culture been influenced by religion? What are the great world religions? How do they differ in beliefs and in ways of worship?

At the end, the teacher said: "I now find myself wonder-

* Mary F. Noecker, "Study of the Great Religions." *Michigan Education Journal*, v. 30 (Sept. 1952).

The American Association of Colleges for Teachers' Education has had a committee working on "teacher education and religion" and the committee has considered actual conditions at several teachers' colleges. The idea is a good and necessary one, but it seems that the committee, existing for several years, is unable to come up with any notable findings or plans.

ing why I was so hesitant to undertake such a study, for I consider it *one of the most successful experiments of my many years of teaching."*

Matters so far featured are possible within the schools and can be aimed at the good of the nation as well as the good of the child. Each suggestion makes sense for schools of all types. Today we cannot deny that some such set of procedures is a necessary part of social education in a democracy and of any liberal education.

Next we take up the most obvious thing to do within the schools and for the common good as well as for the child's good. It is to establish, encourage and perfect the religious and church-related schools which are simply free to teach religion. If the teaching of religion could be beneficent, and if these schools can teach religion, let us have the courage to give them any needed boost within our reach. A denominational school should make itself free to teach not only its own religion, but to teach religion in a comprehensive way. We are sure that all the better students would respond, and that the result would be beneficent for them and for America. On the college level, it is a joy for students to begin to open their eyes to the whole human scene, to see the glory of man as knower and scientist, as artist, as builder, as community man, as war-maker and peace-lover, as pursuer of freedom and truth and beauty, as struggling animal under many tensions and pressures, and as the worshipping animal. Business students are tired of meaningless Dale Carnegie courses, and science and engineering students are tired of atomistic specialization and are glad to see the unified and comprehensive. All want to see man and to be able to judge man. And within the whole complex of things to be studied, students deserve the chance to see the worshipping animal operating not merely among Jews or Christians, but, so far as their age, the time at their disposal and their teachers' competence permit, among all peoples at all levels of culture.

Private schools are not only allowed to exist, but none are more allowed to exist. We mean allowed in the most fundamental sense, allowed by nature and not simply by state or courts. But they are not even allowable if they are muddled or mummified, incompetent and unscientific on any important question and least of all on so basic a question as religion and so sacred a thing as people's freedom and people's beliefs.

From the days of Horace Mann to our own day, a sincere effort has repeatedly been made to meet the higher spiritual life of students in American public schools. We have often hoped, and our fellow citizens do not give up hope, that the need could be met by a substitutional program of "moral and spiritual values." It was felt that this program, well worked out, was all we might dare to aspire to in our free country, and it was felt that this might after all suffice. It has been shown in a careful study * that Horace Mann, W. R. Harris and John Dewey in effect formed a sort of tandem team in this regard. It was thought by these three philosophers of education, and perhaps more or less consciously felt by many patrons of the schools, that a pattern of values not committed to any religion and not even to religion in general could be worked out and could be geared into the public school system. Horace Mann himself (1796-1859) thought, however, that character values must be rooted in religion: "the union in the classroom of morality and what he called 'true' religion." He wanted instruction in public schools in the common-core Protestant truths, those truths common to all Protestant religions, but with

* Neil Gerard McCluskey, *Public Schools and Moral Education*. The Influence of Horace Mann, William Torrey Harris and John Dewey. New York: Columbia University Press, 1958; see pp. 259-271.

favor to no particular one of them; as he put it, "a 'non-sectarian,' biblically based, liberal Protestant Christianity for the common schools."

W. T. Harris, Hegelian philosopher (1835-1908), held that the public school is incompetent to teach religious truth or even so much as Bible-reading. He thought that religious training must be left one hundred per cent to the church, and that to promote a "nonsectarian" religion in schools, as Mann wanted to do, would be to promote another sectarian religion. John Dewey (1859-1952) saw education as the servant of the political community, this community itself as advisedly democratic, and democracy as a "spiritual community." Christopher Dawson has summed up Dewey on this point: "Thus every child is a potential member of the democratic church, and it is the function of education to actualize his membership and to widen his powers of participation." *

The report of the NEA on Moral and Spiritual Values in the Public Schools (1951) † was a great effort to do something about the lack of religion in public schools and the lack of anything like an agreed common moral theory in those schools and about the lack also of any common core of values which schools might hope to inculcate. We are far from damning the Report with faint praise when we say it did well to declare that, without preaching or proselytizing, the public school can teach *about* religion, and that the unity of our nation and our understanding of other nations and "respect for the rich traditions of all humanity" would be enhanced by instruction in religious

---

* Christopher Dawson, "Education and the State," *Commonweal*, v. 65 (Jan. 25, 1957), p. 424.

† Educational Policies Commission of the NEA and the American Association of School Administrators, Washington, D.C., 1951.

matters. This, so far, we would put down as the factual study of religion in public schools.

This interesting report then seems to us to bog down. It gets into a fix that is really a dilemma. It reports that the American people "have rightly expected" the schools to teach moral and spiritual values and that the schools "have a highly significant function in teaching moral and spiritual values." The difficulty, and we think the men making the report did not sufficiently see this, is that in the public school these values can only be taught on a "nonsectarian" basis. And this, as Harris pointed out, means promoting a new sect, the naturalistic sect surely not wanted by Mann, probably not wanted by Harris, but certainly wanted by Dewey; a sect which, as Justice Douglas implied in the Zorach case, is in fact a foreigner and intruder in American society. The nonsectarian approach runs almost at once into a secularist religion. Anyone at all acquainted with the history of America would guess that just such a result would accrue, and John Dewey, declaring so vehemently, in A Common Faith, for a secular religion, saw that such must be the issue of the "nonsectarian" approach, in school and in society. The men making the 1951 report on values in the schools were less perceptive than Dewey. Let us sum up the difficulty and dilemma in the words of Philip H. Phenix *:

It seems unfortunately to be the case that what has been presented as a means for preserving religious peace and freedom through secularization has to some extent become a method for propagating a particular dogmatic faith, namely, scientific naturalism or, to give it another name, naturalistic humanism.

* Philip H. Phenix, "Religion in American Public School Education." Teachers College Record, v. 57 (Oct. 1955), p. 30.

As just said, we are in a fix or a "pickle." There is no easy and straight road to outlining feasible religious and moral values for the public schools, though of course some values are always being effected by everything public: by sports, by TV, by movies, by the Army. Perhaps the best over-all attempt up to this time to bring together a plan for the values we may hope to achieve in public schools is that embodied in the Kentucky Plan, which aims at once to teach about religion and to inculcate values. We shall use the summary of it made by William C. Bower [*] who puts it down as saying in part that the school should:

1. provide the child with actual experience of moral and spiritual values, a) as these arise in the relations and activities of the school, and b) as they occur in subject matters of the curriculum;
2. give the student an understanding of the relation of religion to the development of both historical and contemporary culture;
3. create respect for the various forms of religious beliefs and practices, through an understanding of their origins;
4. give the student an understanding and appreciation of religion as expressed in the local community;
5. respect the values, religious and other, by which people live; and
6. let the churches take over from there, and, as they see fit, work out interpretations and achieve commitments to beliefs and practices.

[*] William Clayton Bower, "A Proposed Program." *Religious Education*, v. 50 (July-Aug. 1955), p. 214. See also Dr. Bower's *Church and State in Education*, Chicago Univ. Press, 1944; the two chapters "Toward a Constructive Solution," though now somewhat out of date, are very useful, as is the volume on the Kentucky Plan, *Moral Values in Public Education*, by Ellis Ford Hartford, Harper, 1958.

To succeed in teaching religion in spite of the supposed difficulty of the "separation principle," several expedients have been suggested and some of them tried. Jews have sometimes asked for at least a decent allotment of time so that the public school would not keep eating up the child's day and week; then religion could be taught in church and synagogue. Still, this is a method of teaching religion in spite of and not because of the school and through the school's regular operation.

The most famous expedient and experiment has been "released time," sometimes called the Gary Plan because it originated in Gary, Indiana, a generation ago. Children are allowed an hour a week for religious instruction. One way is for children and teachers to use public school properties, tax-supported, and assemble by religions for instruction in religion by presumably competent co-religionists. The practice of such teaching grew up rapidly, especially among Protestants, during the generation preceding the McCollum decision (1948). That decision by the U.S. Supreme Court cramped and nearly killed the practice, but the practice has now been in some sporadic ways resumed, e.g., by Catholics and Protestants during the noon recess in a Michigan public high school.

Released time never was or will be a solution. At best, it reached a fraction in public schools and in a kind of hole-in-the-corner way; it is "at best," says F. Ernest Johnson, "an effort to compensate a defect . . . providing religious education in this marginal, supplementary fashion." Teachers of religion marched into the school once a week, and, practically in spite of the school, imported a modicum of religious instruction.

Things had come to a desperate pass when we made a to-do over released time. Protestants took best to it, partly because as a rule they are short on church schools and

partly from an inveterate feeling that the public schools
are theirs, that this is a Protestant country and that anything
derogatory to public schools such as the hint that they tend
to secularism is an attack on the Protestant church, state
and school. As Dr. Johnson says, it was hoped that released
time could be stretched to cover a serious defect in the
schools. The National Council of Churches in its 1952
declaration against secularism in education indicated a
change in the direction of realism.

Another way to use released or "dismissed" time, a way
used for example in New York State and in Providence,
R.I., is to allow children, at their parents' written request,
to leave school an hour a week to be instructed in religion
somewhere off the school premises. In regard to this type
of "released" time, the U.S. Supreme Court declared favor-
ably in the Zorach case and said that the idea of adjusting
the schedule of events to the wishes and needs of the people
is entirely within American tradition.

By this method a few children, sometimes more than ten
per cent, receive some instruction in religion in spite of
the schools, not on account of them and in and through
the regular working of schools. This technique helps in the
sense that it is at least an official recognition of both a
need and a right. But in practice, "dismissed" time is a
poor substitute for regular instruction in religion. Even on
the New York legally-blessed plan for released time, it takes
a lot of good will and cooperation to achieve a little. We
do say, however, that with that good will and cooperation
something far better than standing by is being done in
various cities of New York State. We know that released
time has worked well among Catholics in Ithaca, Watkins
Glen, and Fairport; and New York City Catholics are making something of it, though, strangely enough, Protestants
in that city have rather generally dropped released time.

On the whole, we believe the success is far from phenomenal. When we consider the total body of church-minded parents and children in America, even in New York State the result is on the meager side, and in the nation it is as nothing. The instruction thus reaching a tiny fraction of our school population is, in any event, done in spite of the schools, and we cannot think that it will take us far toward solving our major educational, cultural and religious problems, our juvenile problems, or any important problems of America and the world.

Grant then that religious instruction in and through and on account of the schools, public and private, would be a good thing for the child and the nation. About released time in this regard let us be modest. Released time of the condemned Champaign-McCollum type did not take us far in that direction, and released or "dismissed" time of the approved Zorach type, though it gives us a hand, will not take us nearly far enough. The latter adds up to the barest minimum, and the two of them at their level best leave us radically with a problem to be solved. To begin to do anything notable about the problem we must turn to some better solution.

We thus come back to the church-related school and to the private school of any type. So far as the teaching of religion in school is concerned, obviously the best way is to work in and through and with the church-related school and in general with the private school. For several reasons, this also presents some difficulties. For one thing, most children are attending public schools and will continue to do so. The Catholic schools are our main body of private grade and high schools. Yet though Catholic school enrollment jumped from 5.2 per cent of the total USA school enrollment in 1900 to 10.9 per cent in 1950 and 11.9 in 1957,[*]

* See McCluskey, op. cit., p. 273.

the proportional increase is perhaps not notable and, besides, is in part due to the proportional increase in the Catholic population. In the near future, with the total post-war birthrate increasing and the Catholic birthrate increasing perhaps slightly faster, and with Catholic schools, above all on the higher levels, not expanding fast enough to keep the pace, there will be more Catholic children, proportionately and absolutely, in public schools and colleges. Thus, in any case, the church-related schools, Jewish, Catholic and Protestant all added together, will be able to meet the problem only in part.

Even so, the church-related school is so good in so important a matter that all reasonable and patriotic citizens will give it whatever support, moral or other, is in their power. These citizens, committed almost by contract (as we all are in America) to freedoms as well as to the common good, want this good thing done, namely religion in the schools, and up to now they cannot think of a better way to get it done. So that is a main direction in which as patriots and lovers of freedom they will be zealous to work. When Dr. James B. Conant said that private high schools should be scuttled, James A. Pike, then dean of St. John the Divine in New York City, demurred for reasons of freedom and patriotism as well as of religion. On the contrary, said Dr. Pike, the private schools should be strengthened for the sake of academic freedom and religious literacy. Dr. Pike said * that people should:

1. Campaign relentlessly for the right of a religious orientation toward life to be represented equally in the schools with secularist orientations.
2. Make sacrifices adequate to the support of schools providing a "transcendent level which can challenge

* *New York Times,* April 22, 1952; I: p. 18.

all statism, all thought-control, all totalitarianism, all earth-bound conceptions of man's destiny."

3. Increase the availability of such education to families on all income levels.

4. Influence private preparatory schools to communicate this view of life, and see that private universities allow the Judeo-Christian tradition a hearing, "an end required by true academic freedom."

5. Make increasingly evident the relation of religion to democracy.

Even more remarkable as a gesture and as fact in helping a private school and the whole community was the act performed in 1953 by Jews in Toledo, Ohio, who bought a coveted piece of land and gave a generous portion of it to nuns to establish a school.

Private schools of religious orientation are American to the core, and have on them the highest stamp of legal blessing. These schools are wanted by some people and are good for children and the nation. It follows that both private citizens and the state should, for the sake of freedom and the common good, encourage those schools, and, as lovers of freedom and the common good, those engaged in the public schools should encourage private schools. The form of official or unofficial encouragement is another question. Catholic leaders keep saying that since these schools express the free choice of many and do a good and approved work, children in them should obtain "supplementary services," also called "welfare services," out of tax money. Some persons and groups will continue to be irate at the suggestion; they say that any such practice violates the principle of "separation" of church and state, and is an opening wedge. As we saw, the Supreme Court has taken up cases, for example in New Jersey and Louisiana, and said that it does not violate the Constitution to use "our" tax money to transport children to school or to furnish them textbooks in non-religious subjects.

We must mention the fact, too, that several democratic Western nations have been monetarily aiding private, church-related education in various ways and degrees. A discussion of the implied and encountered problems was conducted in 1955 by representatives from ten nations, who said in part: justice demands that these schools receive a share of public funds; that equal salaries be made available to teachers in public and private schools; and equal recognition be accorded to degrees so long as these are given by approved schools. The dilemma faced by democratic nations, they continued, is this: these nations "affirm the formal and juridical democratic right of liberty of education but effectively deny that right by refusing the material conditions for its exercise." Denial of parity, said a leader in the discussions, is a "feudal and Jacobin concept."

There does occur a lack of equity and lack of justice, said these representatives of the Union Internationale Pour La Liberté D'enseignement. Yet on the whole the nations for which they spoke treat church-related schools far more handsomely than we yet feel free to do. Take these instances:

Belgium: the greatest lack of equity in Europe for private schools.

Holland: "complete equality" between Catholic and Protestant schools.

Scotland: Catholic and Protestant schools receive 100 per cent maintenance costs and 100 per cent for replacement and expansion.

England: 90 per cent for maintenance, 50 per cent for replacement, nothing for expansion of church-related schools.

France: 1.2 per cent of the education budget goes to the church-related schools, though these form more than 25 per cent of all schools.

Italy: something is allowed for children six to ten years old in church-related schools; otherwise nothing, not even tax exemption.

West Germany: salaries are state-paid to teachers in Catholic and Protestant confessional schools.*

Two considerable difficulties remain unfaced and of course unsolved. One is that it is hard to know where to draw the line. It is hard to say where the "supplementary" and "welfare" services for the good of the child and the nation leave off and the support of a particular religion begins; and yet those goods are integral to the common good, without which we perish. Presumably that narrow-line question will recur for the courts. Put it this way. If for his good and the nation's good, it is just and good to furnish the child a ride to any approved school on our roads with our money, and to furnish him books and milk and hot lunch and polio shots, perhaps for his good and the nation's good it would be just and good to furnish him the best types of lighting and heating while he studies and of playgrounds while he plays. Whether the school is "private" rather than "public" would be irrelevant. This helping would primarily be helping the child and the common good of the nation, and therefore we could not afford, nor would it be right, not to do it. But secondarily it might conceivably in some instances help a particular

* See Robert Drinan, S.J., "Ten Nations Discuss Freedom of Education." *America*, v. 93 (Sept. 3, 1955), pp. 526-528. In 1959, Belgium corrected the earlier unbalance, as France also did.

religion such as Lutheran or Dutch Reformed or Catholic. Anyone can readily go on naming other "welfare" and "supplementary" services that might help the child and the common good and at the same time happen to help a family, a business or a church. The argument that helping the child and the nation, if it incidentally helps a religion, is evil because it amounts to an "opening wedge," is based on something unknown and unknowable. We will simply have to do what helps the child and the nation even if on occasion our action should incidentally turn out to be of benefit to some church or synagogue or to some business. We must make our choice—either give up working for and with the common good or take the chance of having our action now and then fall in with the good of particular interests and particular groups. When the city puts up stop-and-go signs, or directs traffic in front of a church on Sunday mornings, its aim is to serve citizens and the city. But of course it may also be assisting a particular religion. It must act for the common good even though sometimes its action turns out to be of special benefit to Jehovah's Witnesses; and in fact the mayor of an Iowa town ruled that the Witnesses had a right, based on freedom of speech, to distribute their literature even though they were jamming up business transactions.

We see no real but only a naive and sentimental way to draw an absolute line between these: between welfare services and some non-welfare services for the child. What would non-welfare services be like and how could they be justified? A second difficulty is that in practice it would be quite a trick to draw an absolute line between the child's good and the nation's good on the one hand and the good of particular groups on the other. The best we can say, as non-absolutists in the everyday affairs of men, is that either of those lines is likely to remain difficult to draw. The line itself might have to be winding and serpentine—and that is just what a justice on the Supreme Bench said about erecting a Jefferson's "wall" against teaching religion in public schools. "Separation" turns out to be more complex in theory and practice than simple, uninformed minds would suppose. But that is true of all social issues.

Drawing the line is difficult because it involves the problem of justice, the basic problem in the theory and practice of education. In philosophy of education we are always concerned with the parents, the child and the common good. A school system that keeps getting in the way of any of those is a bad system. The way in which the problem comes up in the present context is the following. If it is just and good to have private non-profit schools at all, perhaps it should be judged just and good to take some tax moneys, to which people sending their children to private church-related schools contribute pro-rata with everybody else, and help to pay the underpaid teachers in some of those schools. England does exactly that, and so do Canada and West Germany. We must sufficiently free ourselves to consider what they do.

Even a better suggestion is this: use some of that tax money to help make those teachers exceedingly good and topflight teachers. Which would we be doing then—aiding a church, or aiding the child, the community and the nation? That *is* a line difficult to draw! If the question came up, the Supreme Court might lose some sleep in deciding it.

America wants teachers and is in a crisis due to a shortage of them; what is more, America, as any nation, needs dedicated teachers. Here in the persons of Catholic nuns alone, there are at least 90,000 dedicated teachers, nearly one-tenth of all primary and secondary teachers in America, and these 90,000 teachers are offering their services in a type of school both badly needed and officially and legally approved. We would not want to see them hobbled. Further still, in justice to those teachers and in view of the need and the common good, we say that America should do more than tolerate the gift of 90,000 teachers.* It should be glad to help them to be the best teachers they can be. If this means financial subvention, to be used in making them into excellent teachers, the very best they can be, then by all means let the subvention be forthcoming. We cannot afford either to be pusillanimous or to be ruled by prejudice where the good of the child is concerned, whatever his race or creed or whatever the approved school his parents freely choose, or again where the common good of the community and the nation is concerned. No matter what our feelings and prejudices, we cannot afford to let any brilliant, budding scientists languish, in freely chosen Jewish or Lutheran or Catholic schools, for lack of equipment and well-prepared teachers. We cannot afford to continue the present system of segregating our common tax money.

Others have suggested that Americans use tax money to assist approved private schools, not merely with books or with bus rides, but in a total way. The present writer limits the assistance, not necessarily on legal or constitutional or moral grounds, but because at this time it seems to him that more good can be done for the child and the nation by asking half a loaf, constitutionally and morally due, than by asking a whole loaf similarly due. It is pleasant to

* The liveliest and most important recent development in Catholic schools is the Sister Formation Movement which, among other things, aims at: constantly improving the quality of the nun's teaching, and by 1970 doubling the number of nun-teachers in America.

discover that the distinguished Jewish sociologist of religion, Will Herberg, has taken exactly the same view.*

We should at least in passing identify those who are making the total suggestion, why they make it and how they think it could be implemented.

Two professors of Chicago University, seemingly working independently, have said that the thing could be done without disrupting either the schools or the tax system, and that, morever, it is a superstition to hold that all schools must be publicly administered. Professor Milton Friedman has said † that certificates or vouchers could be issued to parents or guardians "redeemable for a specified sum per child per year if spent on 'approved' educational services. Parents would then be free to spend this sum or any additional sum on purchasing educational services from an 'approved' institution of their own choice." This, he said, is exactly what was done for veterans after World War II. If tax money may be given to veterans to go to any school of their choice, it may be given to parents to send children to any school of their choice. The working out of the idea would at once protect freedom and the good of the child and the nation. That at any rate is the opinion of Dr. Friedman.

Professor Proctor Thomson took the same position ‡ :

Must schools be publicly administered? It is obvious

* In *Religion in America* (ed. by Cogley, 1958), p. 143, Herberg says: "I fully recognize the justice *in principle* of the Catholic claim to public support of parochial schools, even to the point of contributing to the tuition of students and the salaries of teachers; yet I think it would be misconceived to press such claims at the present time or in the forseeable future."

† Milton Friedman, "The Role of Government in Education," in *Economics and the Public Interest*, edited by Robert A. Solo. Rutgers University Press, 1955; pp. 127-8.

‡ Proctor Thomson, "Educational News and Editorial Comment," *The School Review*, 63 (April, 1955), p. 190.

that free schools and public administration can easily be separated by two devices, one of which would subsidize the supply of education, the other of which would subsidize the demand. A public grant could be given to privately operated schools as such, or a certificate could be issued to the individual family which it would then be free to spend at a school of its own choosing. The school would then exchange the certificate for an equivalent sum of money.

Professor Virgil C. Blum of Marquette University has also argued * convincingly for the same point of view, and adds the challenging idea that to deny to citizens equal rights before the school laws is contrary to the Fourteenth Amendment. Citizens suffer arbitrary classification because of the exercise of their freedom to believe and their freedom to educate in schools of their choice. Blum says:

1. public protection for children against the hazards of traffic, against the inclemency of the weather, and assistance in traveling to school in fulfillment of compulsory education laws are denied to children in nearly every state because of what their parents believe or think;

2. public health services are denied to children in nearly every state because of what their parents believe or think;

3. state subsidies for hot lunches are denied to children in nearly every state because of the exercise of freedom of belief and thought, and

4. tax-supported secular books are denied to children in nearly every state because their parents exercise constitutional rights of freedom to send children to schools chosen by the parents.

* Virgil C. Blum, S.J., *Freedom of Choice in Education.* New York: Macmillan, 1958; pp. 114-5, 133.

Blum proceeds further than those strong points. He goes with Friedman and Thomson in holding that feasible ways are at hand to enable society to allow freedom of choice in education and at the same time to enable society to pay for the benefits it undoubtedly receives from the education of children in private and church-related schools. He quotes these vigorous words (pp.126-7) from Professor Wilber Katz of Chicago University Law School: "everyone agrees that religious freedom precludes the use of penalties and discriminations to induce or reward religious conformity"; and these (p. 41) from Justice Frankfurter: "Congress may withhold all sorts of facilities for a better life, but if it affords them it cannot make them available in an obviously arbitrary way or exact surrender of freedoms unrelated to the purpose of the facilities."

For the present we are less concerned with the interesting ways in which freedom of choice in education can be implemented than with letting various scholars indicate that it can be done. We say with Blum and others that it ought to be done. As we have just remarked above, suppose that in allowing the freedom and in promoting both the parents' freedom and the good of the child and the nation, we do some time or other in some way or other serve the good of the Jewish, the Lutheran or the Catholic church, or of religion in general. Must we therefore turn around and renege on serving man's freedom and the good of the child and the nation? Of course, the state-church-school question is a hot one. But if to avoid the chance of possibly assisting some religion we renege on serving freedom and the child and the common good, we are cutting off our nose to spite our face.

The basic questions thus come down to a few simple ones. First: Do we as a nation and as citizens really approve the freedom of our own people to found and conduct private and church-related schools, or are we kidding? Second: If we really do approve those schools and the right to found and maintain them, is it because: a) we believe in freedom, and b) in the service these schools do for freedom and for the child and the nation? Third: Do we think it constitutional and eminently just to proceed in such a way as practically to pressure those schools and their freedoms out of existence? Fourth: As Dr. Katz says,* "we exact a price for the exercise of this liberty." But is liberty real liberty when it has to be bought in what Justice Frankfurter has called "an obviously arbitrary way"?

Our question is simple and at the same time ultra-American. We are asking whether in love of justice and freedom and the common good, such and such radical and primordial things should be done. Of course, whatever we say here, these questions regarding justice and freedom and the common good must eventually be raised. As a people, we must begin to raise them. To be much good as a people we must love freedom and justice and must seek the common good in many ways. Otherwise, we are limp patriots and citizens, and limp lovers of God and man.

Is it un-American to keep raising these questions? The fact is that all believers in freedom should be raising them. Senator Joseph S. Clark of Pennsylvania raised them in Congress (March 12, 1958).† His argument was that we want good education, even if it is a Jewish, a Lutheran or a Catholic child that gets it: "adequate" education was the Senator's word, and he said that for this education, federal aid must be provided for church-related schools and colleges. He said that despite all arguments on "separation"

* Wilber G. Katz, "The Freedom to Believe," *Atlantic Monthly*, 192 (Oct. 1953), p. 69.
† See *New York Times*, March 13, 1958.

—some of which he said he would admit—"whether an American boy or girl gets a good education is just as important regardless of whether that boy or girl is a Catholic, Lutheran or Jewish . . . Let's face up to it."

On this point of the child's good and the nation's good, Leo Pfeffer's statements are of interest; first, because they are remarkably clear and secondly because Mr. Pfeffer should make them. For he happens to be a secularist who, believing strongly in freedom in general, does not lean over backwards to defend the freedom of religion. Mr. Pfeffer was citing and agreeing with a decision of the Mississippi Supreme Court (1941) which had said: "The state which allows the pupil to subscribe to any religious creed should not because of his exercise of this right, proscribe him from benefits common to all . . . *Such would constitute a denial of equal privileges on sectarian grounds.*" (Italics not ours) Mr. Pfeffer himself then added:

There is nothing unique in the nonsectarianism of secular textbooks; pens, notebooks, blackboards, desks, and laboratory equipment are likewise nonsectarian, and their use likewise benefits the pupils primarily. If it is constitutional to provide free nonsectarian textbooks to parochial school children, why is it not equally constitutional to provide these other services? Further, why is it not equally constitutional to pay the salaries of lay instructors teaching nonreligious subjects in parochial schools—or indeed, even the proportionate part of the salary of teaching nuns, who, after all, devote most of their time to teaching arithmetic, reading, and spelling, and only a small part of the school day teaching catechism? . . . For, as one court said, "practically every proper expenditure for school purposes aids the child." Indeed, if a proposed expenditure does not benefit the child it is not proper for the public school to make it at all.*

Most interesting is the fact that Mr. Pfeffer does not by any means accept the argument which he has so clearly expressed.

The parent's unfettered freedom, and the good of the child and the common good—that is our argument, and that is the whole point. "Let's face up to it." It will be remembered by students of American law that the argument of the Supreme Court in the Louisiana textbook case (1929) was exactly our present argument. The argument of the Court, as finally expressed in the decision, was that to use tax money to buy school books in non-religious subjects for children in parochial schools is to help the child and the state, and not to help a school or presumably a church. The decisive words may be repeated: "The schools, however, are not the beneficiaries of these appropriations. They obtain nothing from them, nor are they relieved of a single obligation because of them. The school children and the state alone are the beneficiaries." The same principle was used by the California Supreme Court in upholding a law allowing tax exemption to all private schools.

Interesting on this explosive issue are the remarks of Professor Robert F. Creegan, of the State University of New York. † Dr. Creegan says in part:

The presence everywhere of non-sectarian, non-segregated public schools is quite compatible with a generous measure of state support for private schools representing major ethnic, or cultural, or religious interests, of a given

---

* Leo Pfeffer, *Church, State, and Freedom.* Boston: Beacon Press, 1953; p. 469.

† Robert F. Creegan, "Subsidized Pluralism," *School and Society,* v. 86 (Jan. 18, 1958), pp. 34-36; quotation from p. 35.

city or state. The only possible discrimination would be against groups of petitioners so small in numbers that their requests could not be granted without a fragmentation of total educational effort. This risk always seems to be inherent in the democratic process itself. Within the limits of practical economics and administration, however, any religious, ethnic, or cultural group should be granted the right to develop its own schools, and, furthermore, such schools should receive a generous measure of state support, provided that they pass inspection and prove their ability to achieve the educational objectives required for citizenship in a modern democracy.

Relative to this whole matter of possible aid out of our public tax money for church-related schools, our interest is in freedom and in the justice or injustice of the aid, and in the welfare of the child and the common good of the community and the nation.

Perhaps it is outrageously brazen to suggest such things. Yet for better or for worse, the state gladly uses some of "our" tax money now to assist church-related schools. The federal government has always aided church-schools among the Indians. It aided private universities including church-related ones to do research, with "our" money, during World War II. It continues to assist many of them, and as these words are written, notice comes that the author's own church-related university has received new or additional grants: (a) from the Office of Naval Research, (b) from the Atomic Energy Commission, (c) from the National Science Foundation, (d) from the National Institute Corps. This kind of thing is standard practice. Is this money thereby meant to be used to assist a religion and contrary to the First Amendment, or is it meant to be used, as people ought to use it, for the common good of the nation?

Innocent people perhaps do not know that now for several years, Jews, Catholics and Protestants have been using "our" "public" tax money to operate schools for training teachers of religion for each of those religions. This they have been doing for the American Army of Occupation in Germany.* In this instance, who is the Jewish or Catholic or Protestant or secularist Solomon wise enough to draw that bothersome line between helping these religions—which the practice certainly does—and helping the soldiers and the common good of America and the free nations? Where is the Jefferson to help us keep that line straight and unwavering and to hold up the tottering "wall"? As Justice Jackson said in the McCollum case, we do not find a word in the Constitution or in legal sources to help us make the decision and draw the line as to where the secular leaves off and the sectarian begins in education: "no law," he said, "but only our own prepossessions."

Our position comes simply to this. If the principle of helping church-related schools on any level, in the Army or out of it, in any field in peace or in war, and thus serving the nation, is accepted by ordinary everyday practice, the presumption seems to be in favor of the principle. Or do we—this is precisely the question—for Machiavellian reasons want to accept the principle and for perfectly good Machiavellian reasons reject it? Out of which side of our mouth are we talking?

The question of possible aid and encouragement to pri-

* "Character Guidance Discussion Topics" were published by the Army, in three series, in 1957, and it is enlightening to see how the lesson plans, which if "unsatisfactory to the individual chaplain," need not be used, put the emphasis on "One Nation Under God," "dependent upon—responsible to—Almighty God." Chaplains smile when one says the whole thing is contrary to the "wall," the McCollum decision and the Constitution. Even the ultra-patriotic POAU is unlikely to challenge the United States Army.

vate schools thus admits of no easy answer. The National Council of Protestant Churches has said that church-related schools must not expect "subsidies and privileges." This prohibition is more complicated than it seems. Perhaps to aid such schools is not subsidy and privilege, unless to support any public or private school is subsidy and privilege. In some matters we gladly give the aid, in others we declare it unpatriotic, unconstitutional, and make the thought of it a cause for warlike feelings. We must all admit that up to now we have made no effort to achieve standards of "aid allowable" and "aid unallowable," and seem to be guided only by the expediency principle.

Besides, up to this time, we Americans have kept dodging the difficult question whether church-related schools have a right to support. These schools conceivably do a public work that needs to be done in the service of freedom and the common good, and that is why they do in fact receive some support. Also, as Herberg and others have noted, some parents do not feel free in conscience to send their children to other schools. Perhaps they should be forced to send them, or—as the voters of Oregon proposed a generation ago—be penalized for not sending them. But a third view is possible, and we believe that it is both more just and more American. Perhaps those parents should neither be kept under duress to send their children to public schools nor be penalized for sending them to private schools. Besides, it is granted that we need all the "private" and "public" schools and teachers we can muster.

In passing we note the argument that schools are not secular merely because religion is not taught in them. That is true; and it is doubly true when we consider that the vast majority of teachers in American schools, at least on the lower levels, are deeply religious men and women. Schools, however, are secular if, through fear and lack of freedom, the subject of religion is avoided. Some people say * that teachers in teachers' colleges are frightened on the religious issue, are cautious and are playing safe, which we can only think an evil condition for leaders of the leaders of youth.

Aids so far mentioned for teaching religion in schools and especially in public schools are such as could be effected at once and some of them are to some degree now in use. They have mostly to do with the spirit of education and with some of its techniques. Even more important are basic long-range aids.

In this direction the English historian and Harvard professor, Christopher Dawson, has made the most challenging single-handed effort. His ideas on education in Christian culture are so mature and relevant as to demand consideration by anyone interested in the public good. Mr. Dawson is well acquainted with the picture. One side of it is that education has lost common and unifying factors, and the other side is that modern society has made education universal. The latter is certainly an immense gain. But it has cost something. In the process, education itself has been thinned out, and in the Occident it has generally been nationalized and is now controlled by the state. In some instances it has been made the servant of politics, and here we have the naked hand of power invading the realm of spirit and freedom.

We thus encounter a considerable problem, which in part may be put in the following questions. In a democratic nation such as ours is education in a position to work seriously and effectively for excellence? May education and

---

* See Roscoe L. West, "Religion in a State Teachers' College," in *American Education and Religion,* edited by F. Ernest Johnson. Harper, 1952: ". . . the impression of caution . . . a very real tendency for the colleges to 'play the game safely'." Pp. 141-2.

society hope at any early date for a return to common understandings and transcendent purposes? Can anything effective be done? In spite of the almost complete loss of
the old type of liberal education, in spite of threats to the
West and to mankind, and in spite, too, of the loss of the
religious dimension in society and of transcendent goals
and any common values, can anything worth while be done?

In Mr. Dawson's view, something considerable can be
done, but not on today's commonest bases. These are the
secularist basis and the specialist basis. Dawson puts his
positive reply in the words, "education in Christian culture." He holds that this has great and yet quite simple
points in its favor. The matter or content of it is available.
It could be studied with respect and appreciation much
as the old classics were studied. It would be extremely
useful, too, first in helping us to know ourselves and how
we came to be, and also in facing world problems. It
would be difficult, however; that goes without saying. Such
a study would presuppose an over-all Christian renaissance.
Dr. William Pollard has summed up this aspect of such a
hoped-for renewal in words which we think Mr. Dawson
would accept. Says Dr. Pollard * : "If we can come to a
realization of how integral and necessary the Judeo-Christian root of Western culture is to the central integrity of
its being . . . we will be placing the Christian idea of education in the context of the whole broad sweep of the
civilization of which we are a part."

Mr. Dawson has much sympathy with Dewey's view of
education as a means of enabling youth to participate in
the total experience of life in a community. This, he says,
is what education tends to be, and most notably among
primitives. So far Dawson agrees with Dewey. Then Mr.

* William G. Pollard in *The Christian Idea of Education,* ed. by
Edmund Fuller. Yale University Press, 1957; p. 20.

Dawson says: "But whereas his community is contemporary secular society, our community is a universal one in the fullest sense of the word: it is the community of the *civitatis Dei*" * Christian education in a word is an initiation into the Christian way of life and thought. This initiation process went on for hundreds of years, and "it may be said that nowhere else in the history of mankind can we see such a mighty stream of intellectual and moral effort directed through so many channels to a single end. However incomplete its success may have been, there is no doubt that it has changed the world, and no one has any right to talk of the history of Western civilization unless he has done his best to understand its aims and its methods." †

Initiation into the ways of the secular democratic community as the *ne plus ultra*—that appears to have been Dewey's ideal and his final word. But that is not Mr. Dawson's final word, since the person himself, as of course the culture of the ideally best society, transcends the best temporal society. Education, Mr. Dawson says, should serve to initiate men into the trans-national, trans-political and trans-temporal world; i.e., into the world of transcendent and divine realities.

To jettison the sense of a coordination between temporal and trans-temporal, and to jettison religion altogether, is a serious consideration, because "the existence of some social embodiment of the higher spiritual principle in culture remains one of the fundamental conditions of an enduring social order."

Education has its work cut out for it. First of all, it has

---

* Dawson, "Dealing with the Enlightenment and the Liberal Ideology," *The Commonweal*, v. 60 (May 14, 1954), p. 139.

† Dawson, *Understanding Europe*. New York: Sheed and Ward, 1952; p. 242. Cf. Dawson, *The Historic Reality of Christian Culture*. New York: Harper, 1960; pp. 107-8.

to desecularize our minds. "It is only by the rediscovery
of the spiritual world and the restoration of man's spiritual
capacities that it is possible to save humanity from self-
destruction. This is the immense task which Christian education has to undertake. It involves more than any
Christian or any educationist has yet realized." The task
is formidable, in face of the world crisis and in face of
what Dawson calls an "extroverted hedonistic mass culture."

Christian culture on this view is an indispensable subject
of study, especially on the level of college. Without this
study the West cannot be understood, since without this
culture the West does not exist and cannot be studied.
What is asked is that we begin to "study the old spiritual
community of Western Christendom as an objective historical reality."

What would this study require in practice? Mr. Dawson
puts it down in big strokes as Christian philosophy, Christian literature and Christian history, and says that it would
have to cover the following three main phases of Christian
culture. First, the origins of Christian culture in the age
of the Fathers and in the Christian Empire. Secondly, its
development in the Middle Ages when it was achieving
classical form in the philosophy of Aquinas and others, the
poetry of Dante, and in Gothic architecture. Thirdly, its
flowering in vernacular cultures and literatures "down to
the 17th century." *

No doubt such a task is formidable and as Mr. Dawson
has detailed it the whole could hardly be undertaken at
once by any American university. It would require the
assembling of the proper competent scholars, and a reorgan-
ization of curricula, since our present arrangement has in
notable part neglected our Christian roots. That is why
we must make a general and a particular remark. The task

* Dawson, *The Commonweal,* Dec. 12, 1954.

of education is immense in any event and above all today
in face of various threats and breakdowns. But at that,
some few colleges have had the faith and courage to in-
augurate something of the Dawson plan.* They have the
good sense to take it piecemeal. If not all can be done at
once, only the faint-hearted think that nothing therefore
can be done.

To date, Mr. Dawson's is by far the most significant
program facing up to the situation, in an effort to say how
in the Western world students and professors and the whole
society could begin to recover a fundamental and pervasive
sense of their religious roots and origins. The Dawson reply
contains the chief long-range aids to understanding our
world in relation to God. It contains great and relevant
religious materials; it aims at desecularization of both the
mind and society since secularization proceeds on many
fronts and not simply on the school front; it makes out a
strong case for a new liberal education; its materials, demanding a quasi-infinite patience and study, are not to be
seen as dogma or propaganda—a decisive point for American church-related schools, Jewish, Catholic and Protestant
—but as a given body of knowledge; and, unlike Cardinal
Newman, Mr. Dawson refuses to suppose that the Western
world is the final cultural and human universe.

Today we need everything. As Arthur Bestor said in *The
Restoration of Learning* (p.177), for our unfortunate teen-
agers caught in a kind of demoralized world we teachers
and school administrators need to be equipped

> with clear minds
> with moral integrity

* For instance, St. Mary's College, Notre Dame, Indiana. See
John P. Gleason, "The Study of Christian Culture: a New Approach
to General Education," *The Educational Record*, April 1959, pp.
155-158.

with a keen sense of man's ultimate destiny
with both scholarship and a practical know-how.

To brace ourselves and even to think of beginning to do
the work is going to take leadership, courage and faith.
We must have several "basics" and have them together. We
must have basic education, e.g., in arithmetic, grammar,
languages and history; we must have basic science; we must
have basic liberal education, above all for teachers, as the
Harvard report on general education made so obvious; and
we must have basic education in religious literacy. A mere
secularistic leadership, therefore, though it can help, must
remain half-baked and inadequate. The secularistic educator is unprepared to see, let alone to handle, the total
problem. We may not skip over any of the demanded
"basics." To get all of these "basics" deep into the minds
and souls of teachers is the thing to do first, and to keep
doing first and last. This, of course, will take time and
patience and loving care. But if we could achieve it, we
could achieve everything. Then time would almost certainly
give us what at the outset is often lacking: leadership,
vision and the promise of a great tomorrow.